P9-BBO-680

aurora metro press

Founded in 1989 to publish and promote new writing, the press has specialised in new drama and fiction, winning recognition and awards from the industry.

Theatre Centre, plays for young people, ed. Rosamunde Hutt
ISBN 0-9542330-5-0 £12.99

The Classic Fairytales, retold for the stage by Charles Way
ISBN 0-9542330-0-X £11.50

Charles Way: plays for young people 0-9536757-1-8 £9.95

Young Blood, five plays for young performers
ed. Sally Goldsworthy ISBN 0-9515877-6-5 £10.95

Black and Asian Plays intro Afia Nkrumah 0-9536757-4-2 £9.95

Six Plays by Black and Asian Women Writers ed. Kadija
George ISBN 0-9515877-2-2 £7.50

Best of the Fest, new plays celebrating 10 years of London
New Play Festival ed. Phil Setren ISBN 0-9515877-8-1 £12.99

Seven plays by women, female voices, fighting lives
ed. Cheryl Robson ISBN 0-9515877-1-4 £5.95

Graeae Plays 1, redefining disability, introduced by Jenny
Sealey ISBN 0-9536757-6-9 £12.99

Jonathan Moore: Three Plays ISBN 9536757-2-6 £10.95

Devotion by Leo Butler ISBN 0-9542330-4-2 £7.99

Under their Influence by Wayne Buchanan 0-9536757-5-0 £6.99

Lysistrata - the sex strike, Aristophanes, adapted by
Germaine Greer / Phil Willmott ISBN 0-9536757-0-X £7.99

Copyright © 2003 Aurora Metro Publications Ltd.

Harvest © 2003 Manjula Padmanabhan

Caution: All rights whatsoever in this play are strictly reserved.
Application for a licence to present performances including
professional, amateur, recitation, lecturing, public reading,
broadcasting, television and the rights for translation into foreign
languages, should be applied for, before rehearsals begin, to:

AURORA METRO PRESS, 4 Osier Mews, Chiswick, London
W4 2NT. UK 020 8747 1953

In accordance with Section 78 of the Copyright, Designs and Patents
Act 1988, the author asserts her moral rights to be identified as the
author of the above Works.
This paperback is sold subject to the condition that it shall not, by
way of trade or otherwise, be lent, resold, hired out, or otherwise
circulated without the publisher's prior consent in any form of
binding or cover other than that in which it is published and without
a similar condition being imposed on the subsequent purchaser.

ISBN 0-9536757-7-7 Printed by Antony Rowe, UK

HARVEST

by

Manjula Padmanabhan

AURORA METRO PRESS

Harvest

The inspiration for *Harvest* was the flourishing illegal trade in human organs in India. The buyers are Indians as well as non-Indians while the donors are poor villagers for whom the Rs 20,000 (approximately 444 US dollars) they are typically paid for a kidney represents an unimaginable fortune.

The germ of an idea involving this trade had just begun to sprout when I read about the Onassis Theatre competition, in late 1995. The theme for the competition was "the challenges facing humanity in the next century". It seemed to me that the organ trade provided an appropriate platform for discussing some of the possible challenges, particularly in the context of multi-national corporations. The scale of the play, however, is intimate, restricted almost entirely to the four members of a small urban family.

Manjula Padmanabhan

Harvest

Manjula Padmanabhan

The play won first prize in the first Onassis Cultural Competition for Theatre, in 1997. It premiered in Greek at the Teatro Texnis, Athens, directed by Mimis Kougioumtzis. It has also been broadcast by the BBC World Service and made into a feature film, directed by Govind Nihalani, titled BODY.

CHARACTERS
(DONORS)

Om   Twenty years old, he has been laid off from his job as a clerk and is the bread-earner of his small family. He is of medium height, nervy and thin. He would be reasonably good-looking if not for his anxious expression.

Jaya   Om's wife. Thin and haggard, she looks older than her 19 years. Her bright cotton sari has faded with repeated washing, to a meek pink. Like the others, she is barefoot at the outset. She wears glass bangles, a tiny nose-ring, ear-studs, a slender chain around her neck. No make-up aside from the kohl around her eyes and the red *bindi,* (the colour indicates that she is married) on her forehead.

Ma   Om's mother. She is sixty years old, stooped; scrawny and crabby wears a widow's threadbare white-on-white sari. Her hair is a straggly white.

Jeetu   Om's younger brother, seventeen and handsome. The same height as Om, he is wiry and conscious of his body. He works as a male prostitute and has a dashing, easy-going likeable personality.

Bidyut Bai An elderly neighbour, very similar in appearance to Ma, but timid and self-effacing.

Also: Urchins, children and the crowd outside the door. The crowd is audible rather than visible.

(GUARDS)

The Guards are a group of three commando-like characters who bear the same relationship to each other whenever they appear. Only Guard 1 interacts with the Donors.

Guard 1 is the leader of the team, a man in his mid-forties, of military bearing.

Guard 2 is a young and attractive woman, unsmiling and efficient.

Guard 3 is a male clone of Guard 2.

(AGENTS)

The Agents are space-age delivery-persons and their uniforms are fantastical verging on ludicrous, like the costumes of waiters in exotic restaurants. Their roles are interchangeable with the Guards, though it must be clear that they do not belong to the same agency.

(RECEIVERS)

Ginni is the blonde and white-skinned epitome of an American-style youth goddess. Her voice is sweet and sexy.

Virgil is never seen. He has an American cigarette-commercial accent – rich and smoky, attractive and rugged.

Note: For the sake of coherence this play is set in Bombay, the Donors are Indian and the Receivers, North American. Ideally, however, the Donors and Receivers should take on the racial identities, names, costumes and accents most suited to the location of the production. It matters only that there be a highly recognisable distinction between the two groups, reflected in speech, clothing and appearance. The Guards and

as long as there is an extreme wealth disparity

Agents are intermediate between the extremes, but resemble Donors more than Receivers.

Time: The year is 2010. There are significant technical advances, but the clothes and habits of ordinary people in the 'Donor' World are no different to those of Third World citizens today. Except for the obviously exotic gadgets described in the action, household objects look reasonably familiar.

ACT ONE
SCENE 1   *metropolis ; gross*
The sound of inner-city traffic: grimy, despairing, poison-fumed. It wells up before the curtains open, then cuts out to a background rumble as... the lights reveal a single-room accommodation in a tenement building. It is bare but neat. In the foreground, stage left, is a board-bed across the tops of three steel trunks. Ma sits on the bed, near her is the front door. Jaya stands by the window stage right. To the rear is the kitchen area.

beginning: play about media

JAYA	No, but –
MA	Or help him get the job?
JAYA	I don't want him to get it!
MA	Eh?
JAYA	I said, I'm hoping he *doesn't* get the job.
MA	Oh – I forgot! Missie Madam *doesn't* want her husband to earn a living wage – like she should! Like any reasonable, respectable wife would – *motivation = defined	ideas*
JAYA	You don't understand. *about world from TV*
MA	My son's wife doesn't appreciate him – that's what I understand.
JAYA	… like every husband's mother before you.
MA	And how would *you* know what a mother knows?
JAYA	I have your example, don't I? – Oh, there! I think I see him!

conflict in household achieving certain standards

MA   Well – job or not, he's not got wings, *that* I can
tell you. He'll *still* have to climb four floors getting up here.
But – what does he look like? Is his face shining? Are his
footsteps sweet?

JAYA   It's a bit far to see such details.

MA   Pah! As if you can see them even when he's right
in front of you. Now I can see them even without looking
at him. Just from the sound of his feet. His little feet! Like
flowers they were.

JAYA   Oh, please! The way you go on!

MA   Jealous!

JAYA   You'd like to think that.

MA   And rude to boot. Why, you're hardly human!
You must have grown up in a jungle!

JAYA   Leave me alone.

MA   Alone, alone! Have you seen your neighbours?
Ten in that room, twenty in the other! And harmonious, my
dear! Harmonious as a TV show! But you? An empty room
would be too crowded for you!

JAYA   That's because I live with two people who pretend
the other two don't exist.

MA   Meaning what?

JAYA   Meaning that you and Om behave as if me and
Jeetu don't exist.

MA   Don't talk to me about that Jeetu.

JAYA   See what I mean? You pretend he's not here, so
I'm the one who cooks for him, I'm the one who worries
about him…

MA   You worry far too much about that one, if you ask
me.

JAYA   Your younger son!

MA   Nah. The gods left a jackal in my belly by
mistake when they made him… maybe that's why *you* like
him – he's just like you, rude, insolent, ungrateful…

JAYA   Me? *Like* him?

MA   Think I don't see the way you wet yourself when he walks in the door. Yes! Your brother-in-law – ohhh, the shame of it! You'll suffer in your next life. See if you don't! You'll be made into a cockroach and I'll have to smash you *(lifts her bare foot and stamps hard)* – just like this one. *(shows Jaya the underside of the foot)* See? Do you see your fate?

[handwritten in left margin: reincarnation]

[handwritten in right margin: X]

JAYA *(hears Om's footsteps)* There! That's Om. *(goes to the door, steps out)*

[handwritten in right margin: later on]

MA   Yah, yah! Go on – running out to meet him, like some idiot schoolgirl! Think I'm taken in by it? Because I'm not! I see everything! Even inside your head! *(The door opens. Om walks in)* Ah, my son! My own boy! What news? *(Om, carrying a bulky parcel, looks dazed. Jaya comes in behind him and shuts the door)* No hope? Nothing at all? *(Jaya stares at Om)* They're fools, that's all! Don't recognise a diamond when they see one! It's their loss. Still – it would have been nice. A change. A godsend. How'll we manage now?

[handwritten in right margin: X]

JAYA   What is it? What happened?

OM   I got it. *(puts the package down. Jaya stifles a sob.)*

MA   What? Say that again?

OM   I got it. I got the job.

MA   Oh! Say it again! Say the blessed words again! Never stop saying it! *"I – have – got – the – job!"* Ah my soul, my heartbeat! Come, kiss me! Let me hold you, fondle your ears! Why am I surprised? You deserve every success. *[handwritten: job means success, chance to rise]*

OM   Yes. It was quite easy, in the end.

MA *(To Jaya)* Bring him a glass of milk! Bring him two glasses! Come here, my darling boy! My only delight! Let your old mother hug you to her belly!

OM   There were six thousand men…

MA	Six thousand! Waiting in the sun!
OM	No. Inside a building like a big machine. They had… like iron bars, snaking around and around. And everywhere there were guards…
MA	Police, you mean?
OM	You'll see them for yourself any minute now – they're coming.
JAYA	Right now?
OM	They have to check. To set it all up.
MA	Set what all up?
JAYA	You mean it's not certain yet?
OM	They're just checking the building.
MA	For what?
JAYA	Better train your mother to tie her tongue down!
MA	Hear that? How your wife speaks to your mother?
OM	Ma – when the men come, you *must keep quiet*.
MA	As if I ever get a chance to speak!
JAYA	She can pretend she doesn't understand!
OM	Yes, Ma. It's the best way. Behave as if you don't understand, when they ask.
MA	But why? Have you done something wrong?
OM	There's no time to explain! You'll know for yourself any minute now.
JAYA	For how long is the job?
OM	They didn't say…
MA	And what will they pay you?
OM	A lot.
MA	Huh! That's how paupers talk – *"a lot"*. Listen to the rich? They're on first name terms with all the leading numbers – hundreds, thousands, hundred-thousand –
OM	We'll have more money than you and I have names for! Who'd believe there's so much money in the world?

MA   Ho!

JAYA   Can we be sure?

MA   You met with the top men? They spoke to you themselves?

OM   No ...

MA   Pooh! Then you've got nothing!

OM   We were standing all together in that line. And the line went on and on... not just on one floor, but slanting up, forever. All in iron bars and grilles. It was like being in a cage shaped like a tunnel. All around, up, down, sideways, there were men –

[handwritten margin note: peeing pipe]

JAYA   Doing what?

OM   Slowly moving... all the time. I couldn't under-stand it... Somewhere there must be a place to stop? To write a form... answer questions... But no. Just – forward, forward, forward. One person fainted but the others pushed him along. And at the corners a sort of pipe was kept...

MA   For what?

JAYA   To pass water – what else!

MA   Even while moving?

OM   You had to be quick. Other men would squeeze past behind the fellow who was doing his business. Some-times there was no place and he'd have to move on before he finished, still dripping.

MA   Shee!

OM   What could we do? Foo! The stench! The heat!

MA   And then?

OM   I don't know how long we moved for. Then there was a door. Inside, it was dark, like being in heaven! So cool, so fresh! I fainted then, with pleasure, I don't know. *(reliving his movements)* I wake up to find the ground moving under me –

[handwritten margin notes: seems; cool!; interesting]

MA   What? How's that?

OM   I don't know. But the floor is moving. And a sign:

[handwritten: doctor / examination]

OM   *'Remove clothing'.*

MA   Naked!

OM   So we do that. Still moving. Then each man gets
a bag. To put the clothes inside.

JAYA   But why?

OM   Then… a sort of… rainburst. I wonder if I'm

[handwritten: feels like a meat processing plant]

dreaming! The water is hot, scented. Then cold. Then hot
air. Then again, the water. It stings a little, this second
water. Smells like some medicine. Then air again. Then we
pass through another place... I don't know what's happening. Ahead of me a man screams and cries, but we're in
separate little cages now, can't move. At one place,
something comes to cover the eyes. There's no time to
think, just do. Put your arm here, get one prick, put your
arm there, get another prick – *pissshhh! – pissshhh!* Sit
here, stand here, take your head this side, look at a light
that side. On and on. Finally at the end there's another
tunnel, with pretty pictures and some music. And the sign
comes: *'Resume clothing'.* I just do what I have to do. All
the time, the ground keeps moving. Then at the end, the
ground stops, we are back on our feet… there are steps. It
must be the other side of the building. And as we come
down, guards are standing there, waiting for us. And to me
they say, *"You, come – "* And that was it!

[handwritten: reward / adulation]

[handwritten: dehumanizing so borders on direct robots]

[handwritten: light at end of tunnel = media]

MA   I can't believe this.

JAYA   Are they mad?

[handwritten: resignation / compliance]

OM   Some other men were also with me, looking like
me, I suppose. Blank. They told us we had been selected.
They wrote down our names, addresses... and this and that.
All details. Then they gave us these packets, told us not to
open them and said we must go home – the guards would
come with us for final instructions.

MA   But what is the work? The paypacket? The hours?

OM   I'll be in the house...

[handwritten: screening process: people treated like cattle / holocaust / commodities, objectifying]

MA   What?! All the time?

JAYA   …You don't really know what it's going to be like, do you?

MA   What kind of job pays a man to sit at home?

OM   Oh – there was some pamphlet they gave us to read, right in the beginning. Just to tell us to be relaxed and to do whatever we were told. In that, it said that once we were selected, each man would get special instructions. That we'd be monitored carefully. Not just *us* but our... lives. To remain employed, we have to keep ourselves exactly as they tell us.

JAYA   But *who* will tell us? How'll we afford it?

There is an excited tapping on the door. A child bursts in.

CHILD   Auntie! Auntie! They're coming to your house! Police!

From the corridor, approaching footsteps. Jaya shoos the child from the door as she stands by it. The footsteps come to a halt.

OM   Let them in.

GUARD 1   InterPlanta Services wishes to confirm that this is the residence of Om Prakash?

OM   Yes.

Enter Guard 2 and Guard 3. They are both carrying equipment, which they set down and immediately begin to ready for installation. Guard 3 produces collapsible cartons, which he begins to set up. Guard 2 starts to install a power-generating device after which she sets up the Contact Module.

MA   Who are these people? What are they doing?

harvest-crops

corporate name (satire)

GUARD 1 *(To Om)* We can start.

OM What do I have to do?

GUARD 1 Just listen. Congratulations! InterPlanta Services is proud and honoured to welcome Mr Om Prakash to its program! *(To Om)* Sir, you have received the Starter Kit? Yes. There it is. Sir, you are directed to open the kit and make it operational after our departure. Instructions are provided within. Any questions? *(Om shakes his head. Guard 1 nods and ticks)* All right.

In the background, Guard 3 has got two cartons set up. He wears large plastic mitts over his existing skin-tight gloves and starts dumping all the items on the kitchen counter into the cartons. sound like robots / can't go off script

JAYA *(To Guard 3)* Hey! What're you doing! *(turns to Om)* See – see what's happening! *(back to Guard 3, who goes ahead)* Who said you can touch my things? *(tugs at his arm)* Stop that!

GUARD 1 *(To Om)* Sir: we will set up the Contact Module. It will start functioning in approximately two hours.

OM I – I'm sorry, but I must –

GUARD 1 Sir, *pay no attention*! About the Contact Module, all details will be found in the Starter Kit.

Meanwhile, downstage the Guards dismantle the kitchen.

JAYA Who told you to do that! You can't! It's my house! No! Stop it! You monster, you beast! Don't you understand what I'm saying? Are you a machine? Answer me! Oh! *(abruptly she turns away, realizing that it is useless)*

Guard 3 continues with his job unperturbed by the course of the other events at stage front. After removing everything but the counter top and shelf, he cleans and swabs the entire area, then sprays it with attention to corners. After that he reaches into his kit and brings out a cooking device and bottles full of multi-coloured pellets. Guard 2 continues her installation without interruption.

lack emotion

GUARD 1 *(regardless of the commotion behind him)* At the time of first contact, you and your Receiver will exchange personal information. Your physical data has been sent for matching and we are confident that you will both be well satisfied. Any questions?

OM Uhh … uhh… but what about... I mean, when will I actually have to?…

GUARD 1 Sir, any questions to the information received so far?

OM No... I mean –

GUARD 1 Right. When we have confirmed that the Contact Module is functioning, you will not be responsible for anything but the maintenance of your personal resources. Any questions?

body parts /organs
(corporatic language)

OM But what about?…

GUARD 1 Sir! Any questions?

OM No.

GUARD 1 Right. All implements of personal fuel preparation will be supplied exclusively by InterPlanta Services. Henceforward, you and your domestic unit will consume only those fuels, which will be made available to you by InterPlanta. We will provide more than enough for the unit described in your data sheet, but will forbid you from sharing, selling or by any means whatsoever, commercially exploiting this facility. Any questions?

OM No.

family = domestic unit
food = fuel

GUARD 1   Good. Now if I can just interview the members of your domestic unit.

JAYA   I have a question!

GUARD 1 *(doesn't acknowledge her)* …beginning with the oldest member.

JAYA   Your man has thrown my stove into his bag and broken it! Who is going to replace that?

OM   Not now, Jaya! Just be patient.

JAYA   Be patient! While my house is broken up!

GUARD 1 *(approaching Ma and addressing her)* Madam… Full name?

OM *(interceding)* She doesn't understand your speech. Her name's Indumati. Missiz.

GUARD 1 *(continuing to address Ma)* Missiz Indumati... Relationship with Donor?

OM   Mother.

GUARD 1   Have you understand all that has been said so far?

OM   Yes.

GUARD 1 *(his hand wavers. He looks up at Om)* You will explain to her?

OM   Yes.

GUARD 1   Right. Good. Now *(he turns)* next relative *(he sees her)* Missiz… *(he consults the sheet)* Kumar come this way, please…

JAYA   Yes –

GUARD 1   Full name?

JAYA   Jaya. Mrs Jaya... J. Kumar. *(Ma stares at Jaya)*

GUARD 1   Missiz... Jaya J. Kumar. Relationship with Donor?

JAYA *(in a barely audible voice)* Sister. *(Ma registers a shock)*

GUARD 1   Madam, please repeat response.

JAYA   Sister. He's my – I mean, I'm his – sister.

GUARD 1 Right. Husband?

JAYA At work.

GUARD 1 Full name?

JAYA Jeetu – Jeeten. Jeeten Kumar.

GUARD 1 Right. InterPlanta recommends that those members absent at this briefing make themselves available at the nearest registration centre not later than twenty-four hours from the time of our departure, failing which, such members will lose all rights to the facilities provided by us. Any questions? *(He does not wait for confirmation)* Good. *(turns to the other two Guards)* Briefing complete, initiate departure procedure.

Behind him, Guard 2 and Guard 3 have both completed their tasks and are awaiting orders. Hanging from the ceiling is a white, faceted globe, unlit.

GUARD 1 Officer, Contact Module Installation, activity report: Installation complete?

GUARD 2 Yessir.

GUARD 1 Contact Module in operational mode?

GUARD 2 Yessir.

Guard 2 moves over to the Contact Module and points a remote at it. There are musical notes and clicks. The polygon stirs and lights up. A screen-saver pattern appears. The Contact Module moves, is raised and lowered a couple of times, then switched off again. Guard 2 steps back.

GUARD 1 Officer, Fuel Supplies and Installation, activity report. Delivery of six months' fuel supplies for family of four complete?

GUARD 3 Yessir. (*Guard 2 and Guard 3 station themselves by the door*)

example of exploitation

GUARD 1   Good. Proceed with departure. *(approaching Om)* Mr Om Prakash, thank you for your co-operation. My colleagues and I deeply appreciate the contribution you are about to make towards creating a healthier, happier and longer-lived world! *parody of capitalism*

[healthier world for wealthy people]

Guard 1 exits and the other two follow suit. Jaya shuts the door once the Guards have left.

MA   What sort of job makes a wife into a sister?

OM   Don't get confused, Ma. What they write in their reports doesn't change our lives.

MA   But what *is* she, really?

JAYA   How will I cook now? They've taken all our things! Every last grain!

MA   Who is Jeetu, now? Is he a son? Or a son-in-law?

OM   Nothing's changed! The words are different, that's all.   *wife → sister*

MA   But these aren't words! They're people!   *words matter*

JAYA   Are you listening to me, brother? What are we to do for food?

MA   How can my daughter be married to my son? What will people think?

JAYA   Tell me, brother!

OM   It's in this package. Whatever we need to know.

JAYA   Even about food?

OM   Even about food.

Lights snap out.   *company shifts worldview through capitalistic language*

SCENE 2

The same room. Om and Ma are sitting upstage centre. A mat is spread on the floor and they are eating the coloured pellets

*of their new food. Jaya is leaning her head and shoulders
against the side of the bed. The package is opened. Its contents
are strewn about. There are brightly coloured instruction
leaflets, elaborately devised containers for pills and powders
and a number of small gadgets similar in size and shape to a
slide-viewing device but of obscure purpose.*

MA   Tell me again – all you have to do is sit at home
      and stay healthy?

OM   Not *sit* necessarily.

MA   And they'll pay you?

OM   Yes.

MA   Even if you do nothing but pick your nose all
      day?

OM   They'll pay me.

MA   And what about off-days?

OM   Well. *Every* day is off, in one sense…

JAYA   Why don't you tell her the truth?

MA   Isn't this the truth?

OM   Jaya –

JAYA   Tell her. Tell your mother what you've really
      done.

MA   Shoo! Don't speak to your husband in that voice.

OM   The walls are thin. Everyone can hear. When you
      talk like this.

JAYA   Everyone knows already! D'you think you're the
      only one with this *job*? D'you think people don't know
      what it means… when the guards come from the agency?
      All that remains to be known is which part of you's been
      given away!

MA   What's this? Who's giving away parts of whom?

OM   She's just trying to make trouble.

JAYA   Huh!

MA   Who cares about her? Wife or sister, mother
comes first! So tell me – these people, your employers,
who exactly are they?

OM   It's – it's well, actually it's just one person.

MA   Just one person! With so much money to give
away!

JAYA   It's a foreigner. That's why it's so much.

MA   What?

OM   The money comes from abroad.

MA   Really! But... doesn't that mean you'll have to go
there? Abroad?

OM   Ma, no one goes abroad these days...

JAYA   Not whole people, anyway!

OM   I'm warning you now, Jaya.

MA   What's that? What d'you mean?

JAYA   Not his whole body. Just parts of it.

MA   What's your wife saying?

OM *(To Jaya)* Why're you doing this? Why're you making
trouble?

JAYA   You said it wouldn't affect us – but see what it's
done already!

OM   So *tell* me – what? In exchange for your old
kitchen you have a new modern one.

JAYA   You call this food? This – *(She indicates the
pellets they have been eating)* goat-shit?

MA   It's better than what you make.

JAYA   And calling me your sister – what's that? If I'm
your sister, what does that make you? Sister, huh! My
forehead burns, when I say that word, *sister!*

MA   Shoo! Are you a street woman? To speak in such
a voice?

OM   You think I did it lightly? But at the cost of
calling you my sister... we'll be *rich*! Very rich! Insanely
rich! But you'd rather live in this one small room, I

suppose! Think it's such a fine thing… living day in, day out, like monkeys in a hot case… lulled to sleep by our neighbour's rhythmic farting! Dancing to the tune of the melodious traffic! And starving. Yes, you'd prefer this to being called my sister on a stupid slip of paper no one we know will ever see!

MA   Why fight over what is finished? Tell me about this rich foreigner, your employer! Who is he? Why does he love you so much? That's what I don't understand – where did he meet you?

JAYA   Ohh – just tell her, tell her!

OM   We've never met, Ma...

MA   What!

OM   He's rich – and old. That's all I know about him. Probably suffering from some illness…

MA   Then why's he paying you so much!

JAYA   Oh *Ma*! Don't you see it? Isn't it obvious?

MA *(To Jaya)* You're so smart, you can hear God himself thinking but I… I need to hear it with my ears. *(turns to Om)* Tell me, my son.

OM   Oh, you won't understand, Ma.

JAYA   I'll tell you! He's sold the rights to his organs! His skin. His eyes. His arse. Sold them! Oh God, oh God! What's the meaning of this nightmare! *(To Om)* How can I hold your hand, touch your face, knowing that at any moment it might be snatched away from me and flung across the globe! If you were dead I could shave my head and break my bangles – but this? To be a widow by slow degrees? To mourn you piece by piece? Should I shave half my head? Break my bangles one at a time?

MA *(turns to Om)* How is it possible?

OM *(To Jaya)* If you weren't so busy feeling sorry for yourself, you'd have read what they say about respecting the donor…

JAYA   Of course! They bathe him in praise while gutting him like a chicken!

MA   But why must they come to us?

OM   See? *(holds up a pamphlet)* Look? In this paper it says that one third of all donors are left absolutely intact!

MA   Don't they have enough of their own people?

JAYA   And where does that leave you? Two thirds a man? Half a wit?

OM *(To Ma)* They don't have people to spare.

JAYA   And we do, of course. We grow on trees... in the bushes!

MA   Well. So long as they don't hurt you...

At this moment, a loud tone sounds. All three react, looking immediately at the globe.

MA   Hhh! What's that sound? I must wash my hands!

She gets up. The Contact Module comes to life. It displays a young woman's face, beautiful in a youthful, glamorous, First World manner. She sees the globe head-on.

MA   Ahhh! Who is this angel?

There is the sound of an international phone call about to commence.

GINNI   ... hello? Hello?

OM   Yes!

GINNI   I see you! Oh, my Gad! I see you! Is that really you? Auwm? Praycash?

OM   Yes, it's me, Om!

GINNI   Well – hi! That's really great! This is Virginia – Ginni speaking! Can you see me? How's your reception?

OM   Quite good – quite perfect, I should say! Fantastic!

GINNI   Wow! Yeah... well it's pretty wonderful for me too, you know! I mean, I can't *tell* you how much this means to me.

MA *(To Jaya)* What's it saying? I can't understand when they speak so fast.

GINNI   No, Madam! It's our pleasure! Our duty, I mean! Anything we can do to help.

JAYA *(To Ma)* She's saying that she's happy.

GINNI   It's the most beautiful day of my life! I feel I've got hope, at last! And all because of you.

OM   Oh, so kind of you Madam.

GINNI   Is it? I mean, can you see me clearly, Auwm?

OM   Perfectly clear.

GINNI   Okay – I'm just switching screens here – there we go... I can see... oh my Gad, it's magical, it's wonderful! I'm really talking to India – this is really happening! And that lady in the pink sarong – is that your mother?

JAYA   No! I'm his sister!

OM   My wife–

GINNI   Excuse me?

JAYA *(To Om)* Sister. I'm your sister.

GINNI   You said just now.

OM   I mean, she's my sister, you see...

GINNI   Auwm – it says here on your form, you're not married.

OM   I'm not. She's my sister.

GINNI   You're sure you're not kidding me or anything?

OM   Sure, sure, of course I'm sure!

GINNI   Because it's important for us to trust one another. I mean, one little slip like that one and I dunno... I mean, it's hard for me to tell, from so far away...

OM   No, no! I'm telling the truth! I swear on my God!

GINNI   Okay. I mean, 'coz I've gotta know, you know. If you're married –

JAYA   Why?

GINNI   What's that?

JAYA   Why does it matter?

GINNI   Uhh – I'll get back to you on that, okay? Just now... lemme see... there's two more people in your household, am I right, Auwm? There's *(as if checking a list)* ... your mother and your brother-in-law. Right?

JAYA   That's right.

GINNI   Just a moment – uhh – Zhaya? *(the Contact Module swivels towards Jaya, who nods)* Is that your name? Yeah – okay, now honey... I can't handle two people at a time, okay? I mean, it's just this dumb camera, you know, can't look at two people at a time, okay? So – I'm talking to Auwm, well I can't talk to you as well, okay? I mean, no offence –

JAYA   Okay.

OM   My mother is also here.

GINNI   Yes. Okay. I'm turning the scanner around *(the Contact Module turns)* ... I'm panning across the room ... Jeeezus! It's not very much, is it? I mean – oh! Okay! I see her. Hi! Mrs Praycash? Hi! This is Ginni! Can you hear me?

MA *(shielding her eyes against the light)* What?

GINNI   I said, this is Virginia! I'm – uh, well just look up, if you can.

OM   Ma – just take your hand down.

GINNI   Look towards the Contact Module! You know the thing hanging in the room?

MA *(To Jaya)* What's happening?

JAYA   Ma – just look at that light.

OM   The light! The light!

MA *(straightens up to snap at Om)* Stop shouting!

GINNI   Ahhright! I see you! Mrs Praycash, glad to meet you!

MA   I can't understand a word of what that thing is saying! Is it a man or a woman?

GINNI   What do I look like to you, Mrs Praycash?

MA   Ehh?

JAYA   Ma – she wants to know, what she looks like.

OM   She can't understand, you see.

JAYA *(To Ma)* Ma – look up at that light and say what you see.

MA *(looks up)* I see an angel. - beautiful blonde woman

GINNI *(laughing)* Ha! I look good to you?

MA   Good, bad, I don't know. All I know is I've got to go to the toilet. *(turns around)*

GINNI *(embarrassed laugh)* Heh! Mm. But – wait! I'm not through yet!

OM *(as Ma begins to move away)* Don't go yet, Ma – she's not finished.

MA   Since when did I need anyone's permission to go to the toilet?   money – willing to do anything for

GINNI   I'm sorry, Mrs Praycash, this won't take a minute.   £

MA   Nothing doing. I'll piss myself if I don't go right away. *(she reaches the door)*

GINNI   Hey! I didn't let you go!

OM   She has some problem, you see.

MA   Wait till you're my age! *(opens the door)* Why they can't keep a bathroom on each floor I don't know. *(She exits)* resistant / unaware / unphased by authority

OM   The toilet is two floors down, you see.

GINNI   Hmmm. Your mother's some character, Auwm. I
don't know if I can handle it. I mean – walking out on me
like that! *privledge*

OM   She takes a long time to get there. Old people,
you know!

GINNI   Wait a minute – did you say two floors down?
What about in your house? There's no toilet in your house?

JAYA *(bitter laugh)* Huh!

OM   No one has a toilet in the house. Forty families
share one. And my mother walks so slowly…

GINNI   Forty families! My Gad. Well – I'm sorry, Auwm.
But that's shocking. Shocking! I can't accept that!

OM *(embarrassed laugh)* Well – I –

GINNI   No! It's wrong! It's disgusting! And I – well, I'm
going to change that. I can't accept that. I mean, it's
unsanitary!

OM   Of course, of course!

GINNI   We'll just have to install one in your house.

JAYA   What? In this room?

GINNI   Is that you again, Zhaya?

OM *(To Jaya)* Shh!

JAYA   I'm sorry but we *can't*! There's no place for a
toilet!

GINNI   Excuse me, but you'll have to find the space. It's
inexcusable not to have your own toilet! Forty families! It's
a wonder you're all not dead of the plague years ago!

JAYA   There's only this one room!

GINNI   Look – there's enough place for a married couple
and two others – you! You're married, right, Zhaya?

JAYA   Yes, but –

GINNI   Then there's place for a toilet. I'm sorry, Zhaya,
but there's no way around this one. What d'you do for
baths?

JAYA   I – we –

angel that comes into your nose — shames you — humiliates you

GINNI   You – you *do* bathe, don't you? I mean, at least
once a day?

wealth disparity

(Jaya overcome by the humiliation, bends her head and sobs)

GINNI   Hey, wait! No, please! Don't cry! I didn't mean to
upset you – oh Jeez…! Stop, please! Look – it's not your
fault, okay?

OM   It's all right, she'll be all right. *(goes over to Jaya
and thumps her on the back)* She's fine! *incorrect pronunciation*

GINNI   …look, Zhaya, I'll make it up to you, okay? I'll
send you something, okay? Just tell me what you like and *inability | offensive*
it's yours, okay? Jewellery, perfume, you name it… *patronizing*

OM *(To Jaya)* Come on, now, come on! It'll be all right…
that's enough now.   *> juxtaposition (diff value system)*

GINNI   I tell you what, I'll send you some chocolate, *materialistic*
okay? I'll send you my favourite candy and … tell you
what? I'll sign off now. Okay? It's been a big day for all of
us, we're all tired, aren't we? Auwm? Could you look here
for a moment?

OM *(straightening up)* Me?

GINNI   Okay – look, I'll get back to you, okay? And I'm
sorry about Zhaya. Really.

OM   No, no –

GINNI   Yeah. Well , the first contact is always a little...
ah, intense, you know? And I meant that about... the toilet,
okay? It'll be with you in about an hour.

OM   An hour!

GINNI   Oops! Time's up! Byeeee!

cultural psychological colonization

*The tone sounds again. The light fades from the Contact
Module. Om sits down, suddenly, next to Jaya who is wiping
her eyes.*

OM   My god! That was something, huh? *(puts his arm
around Jaya)* A lady!

JAYA	Not old, not sick, nothing...
OM	Oh, she must be sick – or else why spend all this money?
JAYA	It's too late to ask questions now!
OM	But what can be her problem?
JAYA	Maybe there's no problem. Maybe she just likes to suck the life out of young men, like a vampire!
OM	Sometimes you talk rubbish.
JAYA	At least I only talk.

OM *(holds her a little tighter)* I did it, all of it, for us.

JAYA *(moving, to loosen his hold)* Careful. I'm your sister, remember?

OM *(jerks his arm away)* Oh! Sorry.

JAYA   Me too.

Lights fade out.

SCENE 3

Moonlit night, on the roof of the tenement building. City skyline in the backdrop. Clothes-lines, watertanks, TV antennae and water pipes snaking in all directions. There is a sense of shadowy figures, movements in the background, murmured conversations. Jaya appears, holding a small torch to her face.

JAYA   Jeetu? Are you there? Jeetu – it's me, Jaya!

Two shadows move away. A shadow materialises in front of Jaya.

selling his body -simila yet diff

JEETU   Who told you to come? This is not the right time...

JAYA   I had to. Jeetu, you don't know what's happened.

JEETU   Huh! I know everything.

JAYA   So you've heard?

JEETU   Which part? That my brother's sold himself to the
foreigners? Or that you're my wife? The second one is
hardly... news! Is it?

JAYA   But you must come – they're asking for you!

JEETU   They? Who?…

JAYA   The guards. They came again in the evening. To
install the toilet…

JEETU   In the room?!

JAYA   And a bath-shower as well, imagine! We have our
own water supply now, as much as we want and there's no
room to sneeze any more!

JEETU   Or... to do anything else, no doubt?

JAYA   That?... there never was.

JEETU   Didn't bother us, though, did it?

JAYA   And now there won't be any reason for Ma to go
downstairs! We'll never be alone in the room again, never!

JEETU   So what? If we can shit in public, we can just as
well screw in public too… especially since you're now
officially my wife!

JAYA   Don't joke about it.

JEETU   Why not? I joke about everything else.

JAYA   My throat aches with the lies trapped inside it!

JEETU   Here let me kiss it.

JAYA   Get away! That's all finished now!

JEETU   As you wish.

JAYA   So easy! Won't you protest a little at least?

JEETU   Make up your mind!

JAYA   You're all I have, now that my husband's become
my brother...

JEETU   According to you he was never much else!

JAYA   Still. He would come to me now and then.

JEETU   Maybe incest is more his style!

JAYA   No! He's too afraid! Before it was his mother. Now it's this *job*.

JEETU   Ahh – forget him! You waste your time thinking of my brother!

JAYA   But what about me!

JEETU   Why? Now that you have a new... *(mockingly)* husband! *(reaches for her shoulder)*

JAYA *(slipping out of reach)* Oh you! – You're a freelancer...

JEETU *(laughing)* No! My lance *isn't* free! *(squats down on a low ledge and starts to roll himself a joint)* Had you forgotten?

JAYA   And anyway, I'm looking for a plough, not a lance...

JEETU   Oops, sorry! Wrong number! I can't afford any crops!

JAYA   As if I don't know that! And in any case... I feel guilty... soiled...

JEETU   My, my! Such delicacy! Don't worry, I'll tell the world that I forced my attentions on you... routinely, in phase with my mother's bowel movements!

JAYA   Oh stop! You always make such a joke of everything!

JEETU   That's all life is, one long joke. The only trick is in learning when to laugh.

JAYA   Easy for you to laugh! What do you care about my needs, my desires?

JEETU   I thought I was the *only* one who cared about your desires!

JAYA   You care – but not enough! A woman wants more than just... satisfaction.

JEETU   Ah... get off my case! You women are gluttons for satisfaction... that's the bare fact of it! You cry when you don't get it … and when you *do,* you cry it's not often enough!

JAYA   I cry because… because you satisfy one hunger while awakening the other!

JEETU   That other hunger is insatiable. A man has to protect himself against that hunger or he'll find himself sucked dry by new little mouths, screaming: *"Papa! Papa!"* Little mouths with big appetites. Oh no! I'm scared of that other hunger! Dead scared!

JAYA   I suppose that's why so many of your *clients* are men!

JEETU   Not really. It's just that there are more men with money to spare on services such as mine…

JAYA   You should be ashamed of yourself! A man behaving like a wandering bull!

JEETU   Why? I'm not fussy. Cows, pigs, horses, I'll service them all! For a price.

JAYA   You don't need to sell yourself anymore. There'll be enough money in the house now!

JEETU   But not for me.

JAYA   Yes, for all of us. For the whole building.

JEETU   No. I don't mind being bought. But I won't be *owned!*

There is a silence.

JAYA *(fidgeting)* Well, I suppose I should go.

JEETU   Yes, run home before the agency comes to fetch you!

JAYA   Jeetu --

JEETU *(looking lazily up at her)* ... unless you had something else in mind.

JAYA   No... no... *(She can't face him)* I mean... I… didn't bring any food.

JEETU   Ah... so we're asking for credit, are we?

JAYA   There's no food in the house any more! Only those goat-shit pills and some strange powders. And... and it's all measured out, you see! I couldn't take a portion without having to explain...

JEETU   Never mind. As a long-time client, you are permitted certain liberties. Come here... *(He is seated on a step, leaning back. She doesn't move)* I said, come here --

JAYA   Jeetu – there are other people around!

JEETU   Turn the other way. *(She turns her back to him)* Your left foot up on this step...
(He pats the narrow ledge on which he sits. She rests the heel of her left foot there. He puts his arm up her sari unobtrusively, barely shifting his position, looking steadily up at her. She looks straight ahead) Now tell me about this food. I'm told that it's quite tasty?

JAYA *(her voice is thick and strangled)* Yes! It looks like plastic beads but... it's *quite tasty!*

JEETU   And filling too, they say...

JAYA *(gasping slightly)* Filling, yes. It... is. But it's not... natural... it's not real food... *(holds the loose end of her sari around her mouth)*

JEETU   But it must be, don't you think? And healthy? I mean, isn't that the point? To keep us... healthy?

JAYA   Yes... yes, of course... but *(finding it difficult to concentrate)* ... but ... who knows if it's ... *good* for us! ... *(gasps)*

JEETU   Everything's good that tastes good and feels right.

JAYA *(breathes in gasps)* No... no... that's *not* true... it's *false* food...uhh!... like it's a *false* marriage... Uhh!... *false... false (her voice wobbles)* False. *(breathes out, shudderingly)* False ... life... *(pause)*

JEETU *(wiping his fingers on the hem of her sari)* False for my brother, yes. But not you.

Stands for
- freedom
- hedism
- authenticity

real vs false (WAP)

JAYA   No! All of us. If we get sick, he might get sick too. So we all have to eat this excuse for food and live like virgin brides.

JEETU   Good! Now there's no reason at all for me to come home!

JAYA   No! You have to, Jeetu.

JEETU   Are you mad? When they find out what I do for a living they won't be pleased!

JAYA   They've asked for you twice now… they'll cancel your permit if they can't confirm your presence.

JEETU   Too bad! My brother will have to find some dummy to take my place.

JAYA   Please, Jeetu! Please… think of me…

JEETU   I can't afford to think of you. Thinking of you causes too many problems. I'll have to go away.

JAYA   What'll I do? You can't leave me!

JEETU   I can if I have to. Don't worry – your guards will probably know a cure for dissatisfaction as well – just ask them.

JAYA   But why! When there's enough money for all of us!

JEETU   Because no employer pays his staff to do as they please. At least when I sell *my* body, I decide which part of me goes into where and whom! But it's the money in the end, isn't it? My poor brother. Thought he was so pure. But he's like everyone else after all! Only as pure as the price of his rice.

Lights fade out.

ACT TWO
SCENE 1

*Two months later. The same room, but transformed into a
sleek residence with gleaming surfaces, chrome steel and
glass. The furniture is largely of the convertible kind (bed-
cum-sofa, etc), in keeping with the restricted space. In
addition, there are the gadgets – TV set, computer terminal,
mini-gym, an air-conditioner, the works. To the rear and right,
there are two cubicles containing the bathroom and toilet. The
changes are functional rather than cosmetic. In the middle of
the space is a low, Japanese-style dining table.*

*Jaya is sitting by herself, lost in thought, though a glossy
magazine lies open on her lap. She looks better dressed than
before, but not significantly altered by the change in her
circumstances. Ma is wearing a quilted dressing gown and is
watching TV, upstage, right. Om is wearing a fluorescent
Harlequin tracksuit and sits at the computer terminal. All
sport new footwear. Jaya in Hawaiian sandals, Ma in cuddly-
toy bedroom slippers, Om in inflatable track shoes with
blinking rear lights.*

OM *(suddenly leaps up)* Look at the time! Ma!

MA   Don't call me… it's your wife's turn to do the
food.

JAYA   It's your turn, remember? I did it the last time
because your program was on.

MA   Just hush! It's about to end –

OM *(rushing over to dining area. He starts to set it up)* Come
on, come on! Ginni will be with us…

MA   Better get Bidyut-bai out first…

OM   Out? Out of where?

MA   Out of the toilet. Didn't you see her going in?
She's been there all morning!

OM   Why! Who let her use it?

MA   She can't stay away from it, she says! Gets cramps, poor thing, from waiting for the one downstairs.

OM   I don't care about her cramps! I want to know how she got into the habit of using our toilet at all!

MA   Who knows what happens when my back is turned?

JAYA   Huh! The Empress of the Bath-house herself speaking! *(to Om)* If your mother had her way, half this building would be bathing up here. But how would you know? You never bother to talk to us any more!

MA   We have so much! Can't we share a little at least? As it is, my former friends tell me I've put on airs –

OM   Ma, I've told you. When we have our own place, that'll be another thing... but now, when we're still struggling –

At this moment there is the sound of the flush. Bidyut-Bai comes out of the cubicle, trying to look inconspicuous.

BIDYUT-BAI Oh... I hope I'm not intruding...

OM   I'm sorry, Auntie but who invited you to use our toilet?

BIDYUT-BAI No, no! Please! I was just passing this way –

OM   But you used our toilet, didn't you?

BIDYUT-BAI Toilet? What toilet? Is there a toilet in this room? My! That must be a wonder! May I see it?

OM   Oh just go on, go on!

MA   How can she go on when the door's been barricaded?

OM   She's your friend, you can let her out yourself.

MA   But I'm watching my program.

JAYA   Your eyes'll be stuck to that screen from staring at it twenty-four hours of the day!

pellets: inauthentic

MA   And why can't our busybody open it? Worn out
from the tension of doing nothing, I suppose?

BIDYUT-BAI Is anyone going to let me out?

JAYA   Oh! For God's sake! *(gets up)* I might as well
apply for a job as a doorkeeper!

MA   And you'd make a bad one...

The warning tone sounds.

OM   Oh my God! Ginni's call sound!

JAYA *(struggling to open the door)* Tell her it's because your
mother can't control her generosity.

MA   See how your sister insults me! Her own mother!

OM   Hurry up! Hurry up!

JAYA *(throws the door open, Bidyut-Bai wriggles past her
and out)* All right, all right! *(slams the door shut. Om is
almost done setting the table up)* Anyway it only takes a
few minutes.

OM *(sitting down, as Jaya brings a few things from the
kitchen area)* You know how she hates it when we're late to
eat!

JAYA   Tell your mother to come along.

MA   Shh! Shh!

JAYA *(sitting down)* One of these days, when this dream
comes to an end, it'll be because you were too busy
watching your damned TV.

OM   It isn't going to end.

*The warning tone sounds a third time and the Contact Module
lights up.*

OM   Ahh!

Ma scrambles to her feet and scurries over.

GINNI   Hello-oo! Guess who-oo!

OM *(affects a nasal twang)* Hello, Ginni! Hi! Howdy!

GINNI   Hey, whatcha doing?… eating again?

OM   We're just having lunch… why don't you join us?

GINNI   Lunch! Hey, that's too late for lunch!

MA   No, no, Ginni! *(to Om)* Tell her it's only ten
minutes.

GINNI   I'm sorry Auwm but I insist. You *must eat at
regular hours,* okay? We've had this problem before!

OM   Yes, you see we just had some visitor… heh-
heh… these people, you know! Don't understand what it
means to keep to a strict schedule.

GINNI   Ah ah! No excuses, now! That's another bad habit
you have, Auwm. You don't confront your boo-boos. Now
you've gotta learn to control it, okay? You can't help it, I
know, it's a part of your culture – it's what your people do
when they want to Avoid Conflict and it's even got a
name… it's called *'face saving'.* But we can't go through the
whole of our lives Avoiding Conflict, now can we, Auwm?
You do see that?

OM   Yes… yes… of course, Ginni! It is perfectly
clear.

GINNI   Good! That's what I like about you, Auwm! You
learn real fast.

OM   Thank you, Ginni!

GINNI   And now… let's look at how your family's
doing… Mrs Praycash? I can see the food's suiting you,
huh? You're putting on weight!

MA   What's that? What's that?

GINNI   And Zhaya… how're you doin'? I don't see a
smile on your face!

JAYA *(instantly pasting a smile on)* Oh no, no! I'm fine!

GINNI   It's a scientific fact that people who smile longer live longer…

JAYA   I'm smiling!

GINNI   But not enough, Zhaya. You see, it's important to smile all through the day. After all, if you're not smiling, it means you're not happy. And if you're not happy, you might affect your brother's mood… and then where would we be?

JAYA   I understand, Ginni.

GINNI   If I've said it once, I've said it a hundred times… The Most Important Thing is to keep *Auwm* smiling. Coz if Auwm's smiling, it means his body's smiling and if his body's smiling, it means his organs are smiling. And that's the kind of organs that'll survive a transplant best – smiling organs – I mean, Gad forbid that it should ever come to that, right? But after all, we can't let ourselves forget what this program is about! I mean, if I'm going to need a transplant then, by Gad, let's make it the best damn transplant that we can manage! Are you with me?

JAYA   Yes, Ginni, of course, Ginni.

From the door, there is now a knocking sound. Jaya looks around.

GINNI *(reacting at once. The Contact Module swivels)* What's that? What're you looking at?

OM   Oh nothing – just – it's nothing!

GINNI   Now Zhaya I saw you look.

JAYA   Really, Ginni… it's… it's… the wind…

The knocking sound again.

MA *(loud whisper)* There's someone at the door.

GINNI   What's that you said, Mrs Praycash? Someone at the door?

JAYA   Oh for God's sake! She treats us like children.

GINNI   What? Zhaya... Look! All of you – I've told you once, I've told you a zillion times! I hate it when y'all speak at once!

JAYA *(now faking a sneeze)* Chhoo! Sorry, Ginni, sorry.

GINNI   That was a sneeze! Don't deny it... you have a cold, Zhaya, don't you? Come on, confess!

JAYA   No, Ginni!

GINNI   Don't lie to me, Zhaya... I know a sneeze when I hear one.

JAYA   It was the – the *pepper!*

GINNI   I'll have to ask Auwm... tell me the truth, Auwm. Does your sister have a cold? Does she?

OM   Cold? Oh no, no, no! No cold, Ginni – it was only the –

JAYA   ... pepper. It's this foreign pepper. I'm not really used to it.

GINNI   Then, why haven't you reacted before this?

The knocking sounds again, more like a thump.

MA *(looking around)* That Bidyut-Bai is really shameless.

GINNI   What? What was that?

JAYA   Nothing. She was just –

GINNI   You're keeping something from me! I just know it... you're all keeping something from me!

JAYA   Oh God, Ginni... we are *not!* Really!

GINNI   Yes you *are*, Zhaya! I can see it in your lying, scheming little face! You think you're such a cutie-pie, Zhaya... but you don't fool me! Not for one instant! Now *tell me!*

OM *(raising his voice and leaning into the viewing field of the Contact Module)* No Ginni, please! You trust me, see, look at me... are you looking? Would I tell you a lie?

GINNI   We-e-e-ell. I don't know! What was all that about? Why did Zhaya sneeze? You know how terrified I am of colds, Auwm! Ever since we eradicated colds from here, where I live, it's like having the plague!

OM   Ginni, it's not a cold. I promise you that.

GINNI   If you get a cold, Auwm, I can't take your transplant! You'll be quarantined! This whole program will go to waste!

OM   Ginni, believe me. I will never risk your health.

GINNI   Though... I guess... they screen everything that comes in. Even if you did have a cold, they'd never let your organs through...

OM   I live only for your benefit. You know that.

GINNI   All right, I believe you. I'll make myself believe you. I mean it's been hard to read your faces, you know? You people don't use facial expressions, not like us, anyhow. But what *was* that your mother said just now? It sounded like... like...

JAYA   She was praying, taking the name of God.

GINNI   Oh. Yeah. Well, I don't know... sometimes I just get the feeling...

OM   Please, Ginni, trust me. I would not do *anything* to harm our – our relationship. We've known each other only for two months, but from the first day itself, I've felt that you are just like my sister! Yes! I wouldn't keep anything from you.

GINNI   Is that right? You wouldn't keep anything from your sister... is that right, Zhaya? You're his sister, so you should know – does he keep anything from you?

OM   I mean –

JAYA   No, he doesn't. He'd never tell a lie. He's as pure as fresh cotton.

foreshadowing

GINNI   Pure as fresh cotton! Ha! Ha! That's quaint! That's really quaint! You know what? Even if I didn't need transplants and if I wasn't so sick and all – I'd get the kick of my life from these conversations! It's like… I dunno. Human goldfish bowls, you know? I mean, I just look in on you folks every now and then and it just like – blows my mind. Better than TV. Better than CyberNet. Coz this is Real Life and don't think I don't appreciate it! You get to be my age and you really appreciate human companionship.

JAYA   You look very young.

GINNI   …what I meant, people in my country, at my age, they just don't have any worthwhile friends, you know? Nothing to hold onto – nothing precious. Nothing like… this… I get to give you things you'd never get in your lifetime and you get to give me… well… maybe my life. You know? That's a special bond. Don't think I don't appreciate it.

OM   We know you do, Ginni.

GINNI   And now I'm feeling tired, real tired. You just don't know how tired I get sometimes.

JAYA   Is it your illness?

GINNI   I guess you could say so, Zhaya, in a manner of speaking, yes. It's my illness. But now I've gotta go. Okay?

The tone sounds.

her world: superficial, no real connections, culturally/emotionally

GINNI   Byeeee! reproductively sterile

OM   Goodbye, Ginni.

vitality = lively (authentic/life force

Knocking sounds again.

OM   See you soo-oon.

The Contact Module goes dead. Jaya leaps up to go to the door.

JAYA   We've got to do something about the door! We can't have people knocking whenever they like!

MA   Oh? Now you're going to have special times for knocking as well?

JAYA *(gets to the door and opens it)* Ohhh no!

Ma and Om look up in alarm, as Jeetu staggers in through the door. His condition is terrible, his clothes in tatters, his hair wild, covered in solid muck and grime.

JAYA   My God – he's come back. *(She bolts the door)*

MA   Who is it?

JEETU   Only... your beloved son, Jeetu. Yes, I can see how delighted you are to see me. Oh – wait! Sorry! I'm your son-in-law, now, right?

OM   It's not possible!

JEETU   Don't bother breaking coconuts at my feet! Yes, your arms are wide open with welcome! Thank you for inviting me to share the comforts of your modest home with me, your younger brother! *(sits down)* And yes, I'd love to sit in this comfortable sofa… Ahhh!

JAYA   What's the matter? Are you in pain?

JEETU   Is it possible to know such ease? It feels so good that it hurts! You know it's a strange thing with the pavements – no matter how long you sleep on them, they never grow soft!

JAYA   You've been on the streets!

JEETU   Come, come sit by me, my darling wife! Or have you reverted to being my sister-in-law again? Come – *(Jaya moves downstage)* Well! No words to express your delight? Strange... at one time, she used to fight for my attention.

OM   Jeetu – you owe us an explanation.

JEETU   I owe no one anything.

OM   Where have you been?

JEETU   Careful... you might go deaf to hear the things I'd tell you.

OM   But... are you here to stay?

JAYA   What else? You can't turn him out!

MA   Maybe we don't have a choice!

JEETU   Ah my loving mother speaks at last! And what does she say? What music does she pour into my parched ears?

OM   Stop it! Things have changed around here.

JEETU   Really? I'd never have noticed.

OM   And the fact is – your permit to live with us was surrendered! *(There is a silence as Jeetu processes this idea)* Yes. I'm sorry... you had your chance. You chose to leave. We had to make our excuses to the guards. To explain why the fourth member of the family wasn't here. Now it's too late to take you back in... and in any case, you're undoubtedly a health hazard...

JEETU   A *health hazard* did you say? Heh! That's rich! Me –a *health hazard*! My brother... I'm not a health hazard, I'm a walking, talking, health *catastrophe!* Oh, yes! I'm so unhealthy that even my germs have germs... yes. My lice are dying on my skull – see? *(offers his head for examination)* They're just lying in little black heaps.

JAYA   Stop! Stop it! Why make things worse for yourself?

JEETU   Ah those honeyed words of love! How they soothe my running sores!

JAYA   What do you expect? You're the one who left. And now you come back looking like Death's first cousin – is that our fault?

OM   We'll have no choice…

JEETU *(turning towards Ma)* And you, my mother? I hear your love for me has been bought for the price of a flush toilet?

MA   When you reach my age you'll know that a peaceful shit is more precious than money in the bank!

JEETU   Thank goodness I won't live long enough to be rich.

JAYA   What d'you mean?

JEETU   I'm ill. I'm going to die soon.

OM   Oh God!

JAYA   Don't be foolish.

OM   This is serious, very serious…

MA   Of what?

JEETU   An overdose.

MA   Some drug?

JEETU   Called freedom. *(sinks to the floor)* I've spent my stock of years – splurged them all, for a few weeks of freedom on the streets. *(lies flat)* Freedom to lie in the filth of the open road and to drink from the open sewer! Yes. Freedom to eat the choicest servings from the garbage dump – shared only with crows, flies and pigs! Ah, such freedom as you newly-rich people never know! *(He is slightly delirious)* But expensive. For all that it looks so cheap, each mouthful of garbage costs a handful of years off your life. And I gorged myself! So I'm… gone. Flat broke. Burnt out… *(He turns on his side, starts to throw up)*

OM   Quick! Stop him!

JAYA   A towel – cloth, anything…

She uses the loose end of her sari to wipe his face. Om fetches disposable towels.

OM   What a mess! You'll have to incinerate your sari.

MA   And the carpet?
    (Jaya places Jeetu's head on her lap)

OM   We'll have to disinfect the whole room!

MA   But the lice — the lice can get into everything – then we're finished.

OM   Oh! It would have been better if–

JAYA *(stroking Jeetu's hair)* Don't say it.

MA   What?

OM   Better if he'd never come back! How can we keep him? What will we tell the guards?

JAYA   We're not going to turn him out.

MA   There's no place for him now!

JAYA   We've managed before.

OM   Ginni won't like it. She'll forbid it.

JEETU *(weakly)* Who?

MA   She'll chuck him out!

OM   She'll be so angry, so angry…

JAYA *(To Jeetu)* Shhhh, don't talk.

OM   Just think of the risk! We've gone so far – given up so much and to lose it! All because of –

JAYA   Your brother. Whatever's written on paper, that's what he really is.

OM   But –

MA   What'll we do for food? There won't be enough for him.

JEETU   Uhhhh... if I could just have a little water…

Jaya wets one of the disposable towels, soaks it in water and dribbles water into his mouth.

JAYA   Don't sit up yet.

OM   It's starting to stink! Ginni'll be furious, *furious!*

JAYA   Look, we'll wrap him up in a sheet and keep him to one side till he's better. Then when he can sit up and talk, we'll just tell Ginni that he's come back. My husband's come back from his… his business trip.

JEETU   Who's this?... Ginni?...

JAYA   Shhh... shhh… don't talk –

MA   See how she treats him – her brother-in-law!

OM   How long can we keep him wrapped up! And what if Ginni finds out?

JAYA   There's no point getting frantic!

OM   And who'll believe that this... *wreck* was away on business!

MA   Look how she holds him – her darling!

JAYA   We'll have to fix him up, of course. Shave his hair, give him some clothes…

OM   But the diseases… the diseases…

JAYA   Clean water and strong food will cure him of whatever he has.

Lights fade.

SCENE 2

The same scene, a couple of hours later. Jeetu's wasted and scab-scarred body lies in the centre. He has been shaved and grows cleaner, as Jaya washes him and attends to the wounds puckering his skin. He groans occasionally. Ma is sitting to one side. Om is pacing. He and Jaya have both changed their clothes. Om is trying to master his emotions.

OM   Any minute now… any minute! She's going to call!

JAYA   Just try and relax.

MA   I don't understand how we plan to hide him.

JAYA   Look at these sores!

OM   How can you touch him with your bare hands? He must be oozing with disease.

MA   …and him – her brother-in-law!

JAYA   How can I leave him to rot?

OM   Wear rubber gloves, for pity's sake!

JAYA   We abandoned him to the streets. The least we can do is to risk our own skin when we touch him.

OM   It's like Ginni says – the curse of the Donor World is sentimentality. *attached / dependent on Ginny's approval*

MA   Ginni will throw him out – just you see! *(manufactured sentimentality (oppression))*

OM   Here I am, willing to give my whole body to improve our lives – and what're you doing? Endangering the whole project by feeling up your brother-in-law -- *non wealthy world too sentimental?*

JAYA   Who switched roles with his brother? Who turned this family inside out?

OM   All I'm saying is – leave him till we can disinfect him at least! Show him to the guards – they'll know what to do.

JAYA   What faith you have in them! They don't care about any of us, not as people, not as human beings.

OM   What're you saying? You don't talk enough to Ginni. If you did, you wouldn't feel this way.

MA   Oh she's jealous of our Ginni-angel! Look at her face? Pinched with envy!

OM   She really cares for us. *fake*

JAYA   Oh yes, she *cares* – just as much as she cares about the chicken she eats for dinner. *cultural - internalised hegemony superiority*

OM *(contemptuously)* How little you understand of Westerners! They're not small, petty people. *- putting her on a pedestal*

MA   Oh she's just jealous, jealous! Can't bear to think of you being inside that foreign angel. After all, who

OM keeps defending Ginny

warning against CH coming from media

wouldn't want to be inside such a divine being? Why – it
would be indecent to object.

OM   Now, now, Ma…

MA   Who knows? Maybe she'll even want you for a
husband some day – why not? If my son's kidneys are good
enough for her why not his –

OM   Ma!

MA   Why not his *children*, I was going to say! Now
that's what I want to know! What a miracle – grand-
children! And with an angel for a daughter-in-law!

JAYA   Huh! An angel who shares her bed with her
dinner? Now that *would* be a miracle!

OM   Would she spend so much money on me, then? If
I'm just … a… a chicken to her? Answer me that! Do you
know how much she's spent on us?

JAYA   Never mind chicken – have you seen how their
beef cattle live? Air-conditioned! Individual potties! Music
from loudspeakers – why, they even have their own
psychiatrists! All to ensure that their meat, when it finally
gets to Ginni's table, will be the freshest, purest, sanest,
happiest...

OM   I'll slap you if you're not careful!

JAYA   Mind you wear your rubber gloves!

The sound of knocking at the door.

MA   Hear that?

OM   Who is it? Who?

MA   The right-hand neighbours. Wanting to borrow a
bucket of water.

OM   Well, they're not getting it.

MA   Yesterday they offered me money.

OM   Tell them to ask the municipality to increase their
supply.

MA   I told them…

OM   Then why don't they shut up?

MA   They told me I'd forgotten what it was like before
we got this external connection… they started to scream
and cry…

OM   Ahh! These people! No wonder foreigners think
so little of us! We have no pride, no shame!

The sound of the knocking increases in volume.

JAYA *(To Ma)* How can you be sure that it's the neighbours?

OM   Who else can it be?

MA   Listen carefully. There's a code, you see.

JAYA   Supposing it's the guards?

OM   Why should they come?

Sustained knocking.

JAYA   What kind of code?

MA   Three knocks means it's the next-door-right-side.
Two knocks means it's the next-door-left-side.

OM   There's no reason for the guards to come!

JAYA   What does loud thumping with no pattern mean?

Thumping on the door.

OM *(looking suddenly grey)* You're right – it could be the
guards!

MA   No, no! It's the neighbours I tell you!

Violent thumping.

JAYA   …it's been two months, you know! Time to collect their fattened broiler!

MA   Shouldn't you just open the door and find out?

OM   I – I – What about – what about Jeetu! What'll we do about hiding him?

JAYA   If they've come for you, they won't have eyes for anyone else.

Knocking, knocking, knocking.

OM   But – Ginni looked fine at lunch-time – she looked perfectly normal.

JAYA   She told us that it could happen suddenly, a breakdown…

OM   But she would tell us herself! Not just send the guards.

Rhythmic thumping.

JAYA   Maybe she doesn't have the strength?

OM   My God, you're right! It's not happened so far, this knocking!

JAYA   Why not just open the door and find out?

OM   I always hoped, you see, that it would never actually come to this…

JAYA   A vain hope… Answer the door!

OM   A dutiful wife would open it for me!

JAYA   You forget – I'm your sister.

MA   That knocking's getting on my nerves now!

Knocking, knocking, knocking.

OM   My legs! My legs refuse to move!

JAYA   Such a hero, my man. *sarcasm*

Hammering, thumping, knocking.

OM   At least she could have let us enjoy the illusion for a little longer.

JAYA   It's God's will, when your time is up…

MA   What'll they think – this delay?

OM   Another month, another week, another day, even–

JAYA   But in the end it would always come to this – the bill collector at the door.

OM   Do it for me, please! I order you – you're still my wife!

Knock, thump, knock, thump. A pleasing rhythm.

MA   I'll be driven mad!

OM   Would you prefer to see your son dead?

JAYA   Maybe they just want one of your fingernails… your hair… something unimportant…

OM   How could I have done this to myself? What sort of fool am I?

Knocknocknock.

MA   If you don't open the door, I will.

OM   And if you move even one muscle, I'll kill you with my bare hands.

JAYA   Your mother!

OM   Whoever opens that door is my murderer, my assassin…

JAYA   I'm sorry, I can't live with this.

Thumpthumpthump. Jeetu gingerly rolls over onto his belly and lies still, as if ready to sleep.

OM   No!! I beg of you – please! Please! Leave that cursed door alone!

Knockthumpknockthump.

JAYA *(exasperated)* They'll break the door down in a moment!

OM *(sinks to the floor)* I'll hide in the fridge. I'll just crawl along here, all the way to the fridge and I'll sit there, yes…

MA *(To Om)* Why are you on the floor?

OM   I'm hiding.

Jaya opens the door.

JAYA *(off-stage)* Yes? What d'you want?

There is an indistinct mumble. She re-enters.

JAYA   Ma? It's for you.

MA   What? Already?

JAYA   There must be some mistake.

MA *(going to the door)* It's very prompt, I must say!

JAYA   You ordered something?

MA   Yes. *(moves out of sight, off-stage)* Yes? Yes! That's right! But where is it? You haven't brought it? It hasn't come? You'll bring it tomorrow? When? Ah... Okay. No, no, I'll be at home… and sign here? No payment? Oh. Okay. Right. I'll be waiting.

She re-enters and shuts the door behind her.

JAYA   Ma? What was all that?

MA   Oh... Just something I've ordered.

JAYA   Ordered!

MA   Something I saw on TV.

JAYA   But... how did you place the order?

MA   That thing, the remote – you press some buttons and you can buy things, do things and they bring it right to the door! But Madam wouldn't know, would she? Too high and mighty to watch TV!

JAYA *(as she locks the door again)* But what have you ordered? How much will it cost?

MA   You'll see, when it comes!

Lights fade.

SCENE 3

Om is lying in a foetal position on the floor, stage front. Jeetu is sitting at the table. His head is shaved and he is wearing Om's track suit. Jaya and Ma are sitting beside Om.

JAYA   He doesn't seem to hear anything I say.

MA   He's a good boy. He's just tired, that's all.

JAYA   But what'll we do! Ginni notices everything!

MA   She'll understand.

JAYA   Huh!

MA   You're just jealous of her. You don't see what a good, kind, generous, loving person she really is. It's a reflection on you, but of course, you're too fancy to care.

JAYA   Please! This is no time to be criticising me!

MA   Who's criticising? I'm just pointing out some simple truths.

JAYA   Come on, Om... get up! This'll never do.

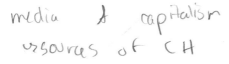

media & capitalism
resources of CH

MA   Want to watch TV? There's something good on in twenty minutes.

JAYA   It's so typical. He can't face things. He never could.

MA   You should watch more TV. You could learn so much…

JAYA   It's amazing that he got this job at all.

MA   On *'Happy Families'* you can see it, the exact same situation. The mother has one son and one daughter and the son gets an expensive job… *value system dictated*

JAYA   Ma, you have two sons!   *by media*

MA   But the daughter is jealous! She can't bear to see her brother succeeding, getting all the praise from the mother! The poor mother was widowed in early life and has to struggle but then one day the father comes back!

JAYA   I thought you just said he was dead?

MA   No, I never! I said the mother was widowed… meaning, she just thought the husband was dead.

JAYA   Oh, it's all so pointless! Any moment now, you won't have a TV to watch!

MA   What!

JAYA   …this whole dream will come crashing down around us! The guards will come and take everything back!

MA   No!

JAYA   What d'you think – it's your birthright? To have all this water, these gadgets? The moment Ginni finds out what's happened to her little pet, she'll have the place emptied.

MA   Shoo! Such dirty lies!

JAYA   And how'll I cook without a stove?

MA   I'll slap you if you talk like that! Why, my son said so himself… we'll be rich for ever and ever.

JAYA   Look at your son, Ma! Look! He's been reduced to a cabbage!

reality reshaped by interplanta [handwritten margin note]

MA   At least a cabbage doesn't talk back!

JAYA   Oh! At least before there was nothing to lose!

JEETU   Why? You used to have a smile before. You've certainly lost that.

JAYA   Oh shut up, shut up! Who are you to talk! You're just a waster! Drifting about the streets, not caring what happened to yourself, not caring about any of us, but when you're ready to die, where d'you come? To us of course!

MA   Don't speak to your husband like that.

JAYA   He's *not* my husband! He's my brother-in-law!

JEETU   And your lover.

MA   What's this?

JAYA   Ohh! Not now! Not this!

JEETU   How strange it is, to be here. Talking to all of you.

MA   Not that I'm surprised. Nothing from this slut surprises me.

JAYA   Doesn't it matter to you that you're trampling on my life? Doesn't it matter what harm you cause to others?

JEETU   When you've lost everything, when you're so weak you can't even eat the cockroaches who walk into your mouth, that's when your life's desire breathes in your ear…

JAYA   And? It tells you to torment your family?

MA   She always was shameless.

JEETU   That I should see you again. You, Jaya. Lying there, covered in shit and dirt, ready to die, *dying* to die, hearing the engine, roaring in my ears, ready to take me away… I thought of you.

MA   I should have thrown her out from the moment she started making eyes at him – her brother-in-law!

JAYA   And then? Some goddess picked you up?

JEETU   Huh! Yes. Some goddess! A dog.

JAYA   What? A dog?

JEETU   Came and peed on me. Straight into my mouth, cheeky bastard! But he revived me all right. Lucky for him he ran off or I would have sucked him dry! Life is a strange thing. When your pockets are full with it, you throw it away like rich whores buying silk bed sheets. But the moment you've emptied your purse of days, your throat begins to scream of its own accord, like a beggar in the streets *(he imitates a beggar's cry)* Help me, oh God! Please! Just another five minutes – that's all I ask – just another five minutes to drink a last cup of tea – just two minutes! Just one minute! One... *please* God, help this dying shit-head one more time... *(looks at her, reverts to his normal voice)* That's when I thought of you. I knew you would revive me. *(shuts his eyes)* Just the smell of your hair... just the touch of your fingernails...

JAYA   Hush! These aren't things to be spoken of!

MA   And it's too late, anyway. She's already married. To your elder brother.

OM   Who's a cabbage.

JAYA   Om...

JEETU   We don't need anyone. We don't need this fancy prison. We managed before. We'll manage again.

MA   What's the time? Look at the time! It's late – Ginni'll be angry at us.

From the corridor, the sound of booted steps.

MA   Listen! What's that sound?

Om hears and reacts immediately by attempting to crawl towards the toilet-cubicle.

JAYA   What's the worst they can do? Take away what was never ours to begin with.

From the door, a couple of sharp loud raps.

GUARD 1   InterPlanta Services! Open this door, please!

MA   It's the guards!

JAYA *(looking blankly)* So they *have* come for him, after all.

JEETU *(holding out his hand)* Come. Let me kiss your hand.
   Then you can go and open the door. Tell them to bugger
   off and take all their goodies with them.

GUARD 1 *(from outside)* InterPlanta Services – we know
   you're in there! Open up!

JAYA *(raising her voice)* Coming! *(gets up)* I might as well
   get it over with. *(To the door)* Wait! It takes a while to
   unlock the door.

She works at the bolts.

GUARD 1 *(from outside)* Resistance is useless! We are
   authorised to break down this barrier if you do not comply
   with our request in ten seconds exactly. *(starts a count-
   down)* Ten! Nine! Eight! *(Jaya gets the door open)*
   Sev– ah! *(He enters, pushing Jaya aside as Guard 2 and
   Guard 3 take up defensive positions at the door, holding a
   fold-up stretcher between them)* Right – where is the
   Donor? Come on, quickly now! *(He plunges straight for
   Jeetu)* The penalty for resistance is–

JAYA   But that's not–

Jeetu, who has got to his feet, starts to back away.

MA *(suddenly, pointing to Jeetu)* Go on! Take him before he
   runs!

*Jeetu panics and runs, Guard 1 chases him around the room,
while the other two guards stand like goalkeepers at the door.*

GUARD 1 Ah! He's running, is he? I'll show him – I'll show the cowardly little shit–

JAYA   But he's not the one you want!

JEETU *(as he runs)* You fools! Can't you see I'm not your man?

GUARD 1 *(dodging around the others)* Always the same story – no one wants to pay their dues. Come on! It's hopeless to run away. *(catches Jeetu)* There – there! *(as Jeetu struggles)* I've got you now!

JAYA   Don't hurt him – don't hurt him – oh he's sick! Please!

GUARD 1 Resistance is useless. *(starts to drag Jeetu kicking and struggling)* we'll have you knocked out in a second.

JEETU   Jaya! Uhh! Tell them!...

JAYA   You fools! You maniacs...

MA *(reaches out, grabs Jaya's ankle)* Let him go, slut!

JAYA   He's not the one you want! My husband is there – *(points to where Om was)* There! *(But he is not there any more, having reached the toilet cubicle and hidden himself inside it)*

GUARD 1 Ohh! That's what they all say when we come to take them! *(in a falsetto, as he subdues Jeetu)* "Not me! Not me! It's my brother you want! My uncle! My son!"* Huh! Lying scum! *(To the other two Guards, who are now holding Jeetu down)* Officer, administer hypo– *(Jeetu struggles wildly)*

JAYA   They're hurting him! They'll kill him – oh! I can't bear to watch – I can't!

GUARD 1 Officer... I said, administer hypo–

GUARD 2 Yessir, I'm trying sir... I... *(holds down Jeetu's shoulder with her knee and delivers a punch with the muzzle of the hypo)*

JEETU   AHHHHHHHHHHHH! AHHHHHHH!

*Jeetu's body arcs up in a convulsion –- Jaya screams. Then all
is still. Jeetu is limp and inert on the stretcher. The three
guards get to their feet, returning as quickly as possible to
their professional composure.*

GUARD 1 Officers... initiate departure. (*Guard 2 and
Guard 3 spread an opaque shield over the stretcher so that
Jeetu is completely hidden from sight*)

JAYA (*in a dull voice, knowing that she won't be answered*)
He's dead, isn't he? They've killed him. I feel it in my
bones.

GUARD 2 Donor secured for departure.

GUARD 1 Proceed with departure. (*Guard 2 and Guard 3
hoist the stretcher up and exit. Turning to Jaya*) InterPlanta
Services thank you for your co-operation. Your family
member is about to fulfil the solemn and noble contract
into which he entered. We, on our part, offer you our
sincerest assurance that we will do everything in our power
to ensure that he will come to no avoid-able harm and will
suffer no discomforts other than what is deemed normal
under the circumstances... (*he pauses*) Any questions?

JAYA   Yes! What part of him is going to be removed?

GUARD 1 I'm sorry, Madam, I am not free to discuss such
details.

JAYA   You're going to cut him up and you're not even
going to tell us what you're going to do with him?

GUARD 1 Madam: Full details will be furnished once the
formalities have been completed.

JAYA   And can I see him? In the hospital, the clinic,
wherever?

GUARD 1 Security and health regulations prohibit any
contact between Donors and their families.

JAYA   Why ask if we have questions when you don't
answer any of them?

GUARD 1 Right. *(handing her the clipboard)* And now, if you would be so kind as to sign the despatch voucher.

JAYA *(grabs the pen)* There – there – your stupid forms, your papers… your…questions...

GUARD 1 Thank you, Madam. We are grateful for your kind co-operation and assure you–

JAYA   Just get out! Take your lying face away from my door. *(makes as if to push him)*

GUARD 1 *(moving out of her range, as he continues his spiel)* …assure you that we will do everything in our power to return your beloved one to you in as short a time as possible. *(he leans on the door handle)* On behalf of our clients…

JAYA   *Get out! (pushes the door shut in his face)*

GUARD 1 *(completing his parting message through the door)* …we at InterPlanta Services extend our heartfelt gratitude for your family's support and compassion!

Sound of boots marching away.

JAYA *(leaning against the door)* He's gone! They've taken him and I could do nothing to prevent it!

MA   Can I switch on my TV?

JAYA   Your son goes off to the slaughter house and you're just worried about your TV!

MA   If you watched more TV you wouldn't dare talk to your mother-in-law that way.

JAYA *(coming back towards her)* Oh! So I've gone back to being your daughter-in-law, have I? *(She stands in front of Ma, who is facing the TV with the remote raised in readiness in her hand)*

MA   I'm your mother-in-law, that's your brother-in-law in the toilet back there, your husband's gone to work at the spare parts factory. And you? You're just a slut who happens to be standing between me and my TV!

Lights fade.

SCENE 4

Night. The only difference between daytime and night-time is the spotlight illumination. Ma is snoring in her corner downstage and left. Jaya is standing near the gym equipment. Om lies in his corner, apparently asleep. Jaya goes to Om.

JAYA *(shaking him)* Om! Om – wake up! *(He does not respond)* Om! Come on… I know you're not asleep. Wake up!

OM Why? What's the point?

JAYA We've got to talk. To decide what to do.

OM About what?

JAYA …when they bring Jeetu back, when they realise they've got the wrong man…

OM They've not realised that. They've used him instead of me.

JAYA No. They can't be *that* stupid!

OM You yourself said they don't give a damn about us– why should they care about him? *(raises himself slowly)* No. They've used him, take my word for it. Or else they'd have brought him back by now.

JAYA Maybe the part they've taken from him is something small, something insignificant…

OM They why hasn't he come back?

JAYA You're right. It must be something bigger. More crucial. What d'you think it is? His stomach? His intestines?

OM Maybe they've found out he's not me and they've just… done away with him.

JAYA   But they can't just murder someone…

OM   Why not? There are no laws to protect strays like him. He's not officially on their records. They can do whatever they like.

JAYA   No! I don't want to think of it.

OM   …give him drugs and sell him to those game sanctuaries.

JAYA   Don't! Oh – please…

OM   … where the rich have licenses to hunt socially disadvantaged types – yes! That's what they've done with my idiot brother. Turned him loose to run with his tongue between his teeth, the dogs snapping at his heels.

JAYA   It's just your jealousy speaking, isn't it? Tell me – isn't it?

OM   What's it to you?

JAYA   I'm still your wife.

OM   On paper, you're my sister. In reality, you're worse than nothing to me… If not for Ginni I'd throw you out onto the streets. To be hunted. What do I care? You betrayed me. Slept with my brother…

JAYA   You never... wanted me.

OM   Wanting… not wanting… what meaning do these words have? Was it my choice that I signed up for this program?

JAYA   Who forced you? You went of your own accord!

OM   I went because I lost my job in the company. And why did I lose it? Because I am a clerk and nobody needs clerks any more! There are no new jobs now… there's nothing *left* for people like us! Don't you know that? There's us and the street gangs and the rich.

JAYA   You're wrong, there are choices – there must be choices.

OM   Huh! I didn't choose. I stood in queue and was
        chosen! And if not this queue there would've been other
        queues – it's all just a matter of fate, in the end.

JAYA   Then why didn't you go with the guards when
        they came! Why did you lie down like a corpse!

OM   It was my fate to lie down in a trance. And my
        brother's fate to face the knife.

JAYA   …and me? What is my fate?

OM   Of no interest to me.

JAYA   How easy for you to say that! As if I'm nothing
        but a dried-up coconut shell for you to scrape out and kick
        aside.

There's a sound, indistinct.

JAYA   Listen… what's that?

*The sound of boots on the corridor, accompanied by a
shuffling.*

JAYA   Maybe they've come from the agency – with
        news of Jeetu… *(She runs to the door)*

OM   Whatever they've done to him, it doesn't matter.
        He didn't care about his life anyway –

*Jaya flings the door open. The footsteps come to a halt. The
shuffling continues. Om looks straight ahead, affecting
unconcern. Jaya stands back, her hand to her mouth.
Jeetu enters the room, his arms half-raised in front of him,
being steered by Guard 2, impassively. Guard 1 enters as well.
Jeetu is wearing silk pyjamas, white on white. Across his eyes,
and wrapped around his head, heavy bandages. Jaya remains
where she is, staring. In the background, Ma stirs in her sleep.*

GUARD 1 Donor Prakash, we have no words with which to express our deep and sincere appreciation of your generosity towards your Receiver. You will be glad to hear that the transplant has been a tremendous success and that henceforward you will receive every benefit and consideration due to you under the terms of your contract...

Lights fade out as he drones on.

[handwritten: Cultural hegemony - power by changing way one thinks (winning)]

ACT THREE
SCENE 1

Little has changed in the room. Jeetu sits on the floor with his head between his knees, facing stage front. Ma is watching TV wearing headphones. Jaya and Om are sitting on either side of Jeetu.

[handwritten: victimized but into it (powerful)]

JAYA   Jeetu speak to me –

JEETU   Don't touch me!

OM   What does he care what happens to us? He's only thinking of himself.

JAYA   Jeetu, you've already paid the price, now why not live with the reward?

JEETU *(lifts his head. In the place of his eyes are enormous goggles, created to look like a pair of imitation eyes)* This is my *reward?*

JAYA   Jeetu – if you would only listen a moment.

JEETU   I won't listen! Because listening brings acceptance. *(moves warily)* And I will never accept. I will never live with this…

OM   Selfish, that's what he is.

JAYA   Jeetu, no!

JEETU   I don't need your permission to step off the bus! I make my own decisions.

OM   ...only thinks of himself. Look at me?

JEETU   Yes, my brother! Look at you? Look at you with these eyes that were meant for you? These blind eyes – *(hits his eyes with his fists)*

JAYA   But Jeetu – if they think you're Om, then we need you! Without you, they won't maintain us.

JEETU   I don't care! I'm not the one who got this job and I'm not going to be the one to suffer the consequences.

OM   He was always selfish. Always lived just for himself.

JAYA   Jeetu, just wait till we can ask Ginni. She'll listen at least, maybe even help.

JEETU   Ginni, huh! Ginni only helps herself.

JAYA   No, Jeetu –

JEETU   A rich woman who plucks a poor man's eyes out of his head – huh! That's not a woman, it's a demon!

JAYA   But Jeetu, without you...

OM   Just wait till Ginni finds out whose eyes are in her head! Just wait!

JAYA *(To Om)* Why tell her? If she goes on thinking Jeetu is you then maybe–

OM   Fat chance! It's the guards who made the mistake! The moment she sees me here she'll know what happened and she'll be mad! She'll be furious! She'll probably have the guards court-marshalled.

JAYA   You heard what they said – the transplant was a success. So maybe it *is* all right? Maybe Jeetu's eyes are good enough?

OM   It's not so easy as you think – remember all those injections I had in the beginning? They were to change my body so that it could match Ginni's body perfectly. But now they've taken the wrong pair of eyes... who knows what it'll do to Ginni? And what about Jeetu's infections, all the poisons and germs he's had circulating inside him... what about them? Ginni's scared about catching your cold! What'll she catch from Jeetu?

JAYA   But they *said*–

OM   It takes time to know that a transplant has been a success!

JAYA   How long?

OM   I don't know. I'm not a doctor.

JEETU   I'm not going to live long enough to find out, either way.

JAYA   Please, you can't kill yourself! I don't care what she says… I'm not going to lose you again.

JEETU   You don't know what you're asking of me.

JAYA   Jeetu…

OM   *(To Jaya)* Why waste your breath? Neither will he listen, nor will it make the slightest difference to the outcome. What will be, will be, regardless of what we try to do about it.

JAYA   But *why*? When it doesn't *have* to be! When all he has to do is to pretend – just for a couple of hours in a day…

JEETU   Why? Because I'm in a place beyond death. I'm in a place worse than death.

JAYA   There's no place worse than death.

JEETU   Yet I know such a place, now. A bleached and pitted place. Scars and slashes against infinite blackness. No stillness, no dimensions. No here, no there…

JAYA   But can you see me, Jeetu?

JEETU   Yes. I see you. And through you. And through the floor. And through all the gadgets, and through my brother standing there, a blaze of fried nerves, his eyes like ping-pong balls. I see Ma looking like a red bundle hunched in front of the blue glare of her TV. And you, Jaya? You're just a bunch of bright white lines, no nose, no eyes, no head, no skin. When you open your mouth to speak I see a gaping black hole, like the pit of hell yawning open, ready to swallow me up. Everywhere else, it's just a shapeless

sparking madness. And I can't turn any of it off. I can't
blink. I can't sleep, I can't dream, I can't even cry. This... is
what you want for me?

There is a silence.

JEETU   Well? You're not saying anything.

JAYA   I –

JEETU   Is it selfish to want to end this?

OM   I was willing to accept anything for my family.

JEETU   Oh yes! And what happened when the guards
came?

OM   That was different. It was the shock, the lack of
warning...

JEETU   It was cowardice!

JAYA   Jeetu, we've not asked anything of you so far.

JEETU   This is no time to start!

JAYA   Maybe you'll get used to it in time... maybe
they'll be able to improve it.

JEETU   Let me die before I'm too maddened by visions to
make the effort!

OM   Just wait, just wait... when Ginni comes, she'll
make all the effort for all of us!

JAYA   You think she'll take your side?

OM   Of course she will. And she'll throw the two of
you out, for fooling around. For fooling her.

The warning tone sounds.

JAYA   Oh my God!

OM   Ah! Just let me do the talking – I'll explain
everything.

JEETU   What's that? I... I... I *saw* something.

The second tone sounds.

JAYA   What's the matter Jeetu?

OM   You shut up, both of you! I'll explain it and don't worry, I won't leave you two out of the picture.

JEETU   Something's happening. The blackness is lifting... I can see some sort of pattern...

The third tone sounds.

GINNI   Well... hellooo-oo! Guess whoo-ooo!

JEETU   Ahh! Ahhh...

OM   Hello! Howdy! Hi, Ginni...

GINNI   Hello-ooo? Is anybody home? *(the Contact Module swivels)* Auwm? Isn't that you, Auwm?

OM *(running around to get in front of the Contact Module)* No! No– *This* is me! I'm here! Here!

The Contact Module flips up and out of Om's reach.

GINNI   Come in, Auwm! Can you see me? Auwm?

JEETU   My God. I... can see!

GINNI   Sure you can see Auwm! That's what we gave you eyes for!

OM *(screaming)* No!! It's a mistake! There's been a terrible mistake!

JAYA *(intercepts him)* Wait! Don't disturb them.

JEETU *(gesturing directly in front of him)* And that... and you must be –

OM   She's wrong! She's wrong! It's –

JAYA *(holds Om back)* Shhhhh!

GINNI   Ginni! That's right, Auwm... it's me you're seeing
'coz I'm beaming my video image straight into your mind!
So you can see me right in front of you, all of me, for once,
not just my face... well? What do you think?

JEETU   *(moves slowly around, looking at something that no-
one else in the room with him can see)* It's… you're…
beautiful. Like... magic.

GINNI   You like me, Auwm? You like what you see?

JEETU   Yes. And the room! What is this place?

GINNI   Oh... it's just where I live, Auwm, it's one of the
rooms in my little house.

JEETU   It's a palace.

GINNI   I'm glad you like it Auwm.

JEETU   I can't help but like it! Who wouldn't? *(He points
around him)* Those plants! That light! What are those
things there? It's... beautiful. Beautiful. I've never seen
anything like this. Never.

OM   But it's mine, what he's seeing – *mine!*

JAYA   Can't you hush?

OM   It's all a mistake! She'll find out and then what'll
happen? What'll happen to us?

JAYA   Shhh!

JEETU   And you... is that really... you?

GINNI   Yup! It's me, Ginni! You look like you're seeing
me for the first time, Auwm!

JEETU   I am! I mean, uh... we could only see your face
before.

GINNI   Well – now! I'm glad you like me, 'coz you know
what? Now that the transplants have started, it's time that
we talked about the next phase…

JEETU   *Next phase?*

OM   But he's the wrong man!

*Jaya holds Om back. Jeetu is facing the Contact Module,
which now rises above him and glows white as the rest of the
stage lights dim.*

GINNI   The next phase of the transplants. You see, we
have to progress rapidly now and I need all your support.
Until we reached this platform of contact, we couldn't be
sure. But now that we're sure, we've got to move really fast.
Are you with me?

JEETU   Yes...

GINNI   Because you have to be willing, for what we want
to do now. You have to be really willing, Auwm.

JEETU   Tell me, Ginni, tell me what you want.

GINNI   Ah ah… can't touch me, Auwm! *(He reacts by
jerking his hand away)* Well... you'll have to go back to the
clinic and they'll prepare you.

JEETU *(behaves as if he is standing very close to someone,
following her around as she moves out of his reach)* You
need some more parts of me?

GINNI   Well, yes, I mean, that's one way of looking at it
but I – I think you should understand that time is kind of
short, Auwm and we really have to get a move on.

JEETU *(moves his body seductively)* Just tell me what you
want of me, Ginni…

GINNI   The guards will come for you and they'll request
you to follow them away.

JEETU   Anything, Ginni, anything…

GINNI   The sooner you can go the better it'll be for you…

JEETU   Whatever you say, Ginni.

GINNI   I mean, really, Auwm, if it's okay with you, I can
tell the guards to come for you right now.

JAYA   No...

JEETU   That's fine with me, Ginni.

OM   Ask her what she wants from you!

JEETU   Anything you want is fine, Ginni.

GINNI   Okay, Auwm, I'm turning this video session off for the moment and I'm going to ask you to wait for the guards.

JEETU   You're – you're going?

GINNI   But I'll be back, Auwm, closer than you'd ever believe...

The Contact Module moves high and its light dims.

JEETU *(stretching his arms up)* Don't – don't – Ahh – ! *(strikes his eyes)* AHHHH!

GINNI   The guards will come, Auwm, you don't have long to wait – we'll talk again when you're in the clinic, okay?

JEETU   NO!! Don't leave me in this blindness.

GINNI   Remember to keep smiling Auwm.

JEETU   No!

GINNI   Byeeee!

The Contact Module snaps off.

JEETU   Ah – no! She's gone – she's gone!

Jaya and Om come forward around him.

JAYA   Jeetu – do you know what you've said?

JEETU   All I know is that I'm going to her... I'm going...

OM   You didn't even find out what they're going to take from you this time.

JEETU   You don't understand! I was blind! And now I have the chance to see again.

JAYA   But... it's not *real,* what you see... I... I mean, we could watch you moving like a madman, waving your arms about, pointing to things that weren't there.

Om begins to move away, towards the door.

JEETU   But they are *somewhere.* And that's all that matters to me.

JAYA   Yes, but – she's taken your *eyes.*

JEETU   ...and left me something even better! I can't tell you what things I saw...

JAYA   Really? So much?

JEETU   Yes, oh, yes! Of course, I can't see what's directly around me. But maybe they'll find a way to change that...

JAYA   You should have asked her...

JEETU   I'd never seen her, till just now! I thought she was an old woman! You never told me she was so... so *young!* And beautiful. Why didn't you tell me, Jaya?

JAYA   You didn't seem interested... we hardly discussed Ginni at all.

JEETU   Well. It would have made all the difference if I'd known. I saw all of her, you know! Standing there, wearing almost *nothing!* And she kept moving, like this, like that... wah! I could have had her, right there and then!

JAYA   But she wasn't real!

JEETU   She exists. That's enough for me. She's a goddess and she exists. I'd do anything for her – anything!

JAYA   Yes. I can see that.

JEETU   Don't hold it against me, Jaya – think of her as just another client. You were always good at that.

JAYA   Your other clients were only interested in short-term contracts. Not permanent ownership!

Controll what he sees / consume

JEETU   You should be happy for me – and anyway, you've got your wish, now. I'll stay alive, and they'll go on looking after all of us.

There is a knocking at the door.

GUARD 1 *(from outside)* InterPlanta Services!
(But before he can say, "Open up", Om has thrown the door open)

OM   Yes! Take me! Take me! I'm ready to go!

Several things happen at once. Jeetu and Jaya turn towards the door, as Guard 1 and Guard 2 roughly shove Om aside, entering the room.

JEETU   Yes.

GUARD 1   Mr Om Prakash, we have been intimated of your willingness to participate in the second phase of our transplant service!

OM *(screaming)* Not him – take *me!* I'm Om Prakash! Check your records.

Guard 3 entering behind the other two, quickly grabs Om and holds him pinned to the wall, struggling.

JEETU   Yes, I am Om Prakash.

OM *(from his pinned position)* Nooo! He's lying! A lying, scheming swine! He's my brother, I tell you – my younger brother.

GUARD 1   All right sir, if you would just follow us – we're ready to leave.

JEETU   Let's go.

Guard 1 stands aside and Jeetu moves towards the door.

JAYA   Jeetu…

JEETU   Don't call me that.

JAYA   Don't go just yet! Please! It's too soon, they've not explained anything… I… we… you'll never be the same again.

JEETU *(grabs her quickly, gives her a brief hug and pushes her toward Guard 2 who grabs and holds her)* You have your husband to look after – he needs you more than I do. *(He turns and exits)*

JAYA   Jeetu! Jeetu! *(Guard 2 lets go of her and exits)* What happened to your ideals, your freedoms? Your pride? All gone! So easily gone.

Guard 3 has a brief struggle disengaging himself from Om, but he too slips out, slamming the door behind him, bolting it from the outside.

OM   AHHHHHHHHHH! You've locked us in, you bastards! You've locked us in! *(roars and pounds on the door)* You can't do this to us! We've not signed any consent forms! You've not taken any permissions! AHHHHHHHH! You've locked us in and taken the wrong man – you'll regret it!… AAAAAHHHHHHHH! *(He sinks onto the floor)*

Jaya looks at the door, too shocked and defeated even to cry. She looks across at Ma, who is totally absorbed by the TV program she's watching.

JAYA   Ma? Ma? *(goes to where Ma sits)* Listen to me… *(But Ma is wearing headphones and can't hear. Jaya shakes Ma by the shoulder)* Ma! Listen to me!

MA *(holding one of her earphones up)* What *is* it!

JAYA   Ma – do you realise they've taken Jeetu?

MA   What?

JAYA   Jeetu – they've taken him away!

MA   So? *(starts to replace the ear-piece)* He was never here to begin with.

JAYA   No! You *can't* be so indifferent.

MA   Tch! Let me be! Why should I care what happens to Jeetu? I've stopped caring about anybody. *(She replaces the earpiece and turns back to her set)*

JAYA *(for a second she is non-plussed)* That's too much! You hear me, Ma? *(screams)* It's just too much! *(She snatches the TV remote from Ma's hand)* You can't do this! *(smashes it on the floor)* You've got be involved with what's going on around you!

MA   Give that back to me!

They do not notice that Om is sitting up alertly, by the door. He is listening to something.

JAYA *(stamping on the remote)* I won't! I won't!

MA   Pig-faced buffalo! Give it back or I'll – I'll shit in the water-supply!

JAYA   You wouldn't dare.

MA   I'll microwave your entrails! *(pushes Jaya away and snatches up the remote)*

JAYA *(trying to get the remote back)* I'm sick of being the only one to make decisions around here! There's nothing wrong with you – you're not sick or busy…

The sounds that Om has heard are now audible in the room. Boots in the corridor. Om flattens himself alongside the door as the footsteps come to a halt. The bolt is opened from outside.

MA   Let me go, you barren dog! Mmmh! Mmmmh!
   Let me go!

*At this moment the door is flung open. Jaya and Ma fall apart.
Om almost manages to wriggle out but is pushed aside as
Agent 1 enters. Behind him are Agents 2 and 3, blocking the
door with something big, on wheels.*

AGENT 1   Madam Indumati? Who is Madam Indumati?
JAYA   Om, Om what do you think you're doing?
MA   Me! I'm Madam Indumati!

Om struggles to get past the wheeled object.

JAYA *(to Agent 1)* What is this? Who are you?
AGENT 1   VideoCouch Enterprises, Ma'am, please.
MA *(to the Agent)* Have you brought it?
AGENT 1   Yes, Ma'am.

*Agents 2 and 3 push a long gleaming case into the room. Om
tries to go out of the door, but Jaya gets there before him. She
closes the door and stands in front of it, daring Om to push
her aside. He considers the possibility, but ultimately with-
draws. Meanwhile, Agents 2 and 3 set up the video couch. It is
reminiscent of Tutankhamen's sarcophagus, encrusted with
electronic dials and circuitry in the place of jewels. The
Agents manoeuvre it into the centre of the room, move the
dining platform aside and install the device in its place.*

AGENT 1 *(To Ma)* Please, Ma'am, sign here.
JAYA   Ma, who are these people? What's going on?
MA *(To the Agent)* How about this insti– instig– ?
AGENT 1   Installation. Just sign this form, Ma'am, to
   confirm receipt of the unit.

MA *(taking the form and the pen)* How do I know you won't just run away after I've signed this?

AGENT 1 As you wish, Ma'am. *(To the other two Agents)* Proceed with installation. *(The other two Agents open the case, revealing an equally ornate interior, filled with tubes, switches, circuitry. Inside are a number of containers. Agents 2 and 3 set about attaching the containers to various parts of the case while Agent 1 explains to Ma)* This is the SuperDeluxe VideoCouch model XL 5000! We are certain it will provide you, our valued customer, with every satisfaction! This is the nourishment panel... the hydration filter...

JAYA *(goes to Agent 1)* Stop this at once! Explain to me what's going on!

AGENT 1 Ma'am?

MA *(To Jaya)* Can't you shut up? It's my VideoCouch! It's what I ordered the other day!

JAYA But–

AGENT 1 Ma'am...

MA *(To the Agent)* Proceed!

AGENT 1 Uhh... This is the SuperDeluxe VideoCouch model XL 5000! We are certain it will provide you, our valued customer, with every satisfaction! This is the organic-input interface, the hydration filter, the pangro-meter! Here you see the Lexus Phantasticon which is programmed to receive seven hundred and fifty video channels from all over the world! There are ten modes, seventeen frequencies, three substrate couplers, extra-sensory feedback impulses and cross-net capturing facilities! All media access: satellite, bio-tenna, visitelly and radiogonad. Manual control panel, neuro-stimulator and full-body processing capacities – all other queries will be answered on-line from within the VideoCouch self-training program. *(ends abruptly)* Any questions, Ma'am?

MA Hanh?

AGENT 1   Ma'am – if you sign the delivery voucher we can complete installation…

MA   But I haven't understood a word you've said.

JAYA   Ma, you *must* explain what this is about.

MA *(To the Agent)* If I sign this... no one can take it from me, can they?

AGENT 1   No, Ma'am.

MA   And your people won't go till I've got into it? *(she signs the voucher and hands it back, not glancing at the many pages of forms)*

AGENT 1   No, Ma'am, thank you, Ma'am… If you'll just come this way, Ma'am.

Sarcaphogus = living in a couch (defeated)

The other two Agents have attached a power-line to the unit and at this moment activate the system. It twinkles with small LCDs. It looks like a tiny space-module. Agent 2 disconnects the power lead and the lights continue to twinkle. She detaches the cable from the couch.

COUCH *(a fruity voice issues from within the VideoCouch)* Welcome to Video Paradiso! You will not regret your choice! Please ask our authorised representative to settle you into your customised, contour-gel, fully automated video-chamber! *(Appropriate music plays. As the Couch begins speaking, Ma is helped into it by the Agents. She lies down and the Agents huddle around her, connecting her up to various pouches and tubes. They do this very quickly and she gasps and grunts once or twice. There is a breathing mask on her face. Soon they are ready to close the lid)* Thank you for being co-operative! Your fully automatic Video Paradiso unit is now ready for operation! Just relax and let your guide show you the way to an experience of ultimate bliss.

The Agents shut the lid. The Agents seal the edges and lock them. They work extremely fast. The muted sound of the Couch voice continues unintelligibly.

JAYA   But how will she breathe?

AGENT 1   Ma'am... it's a total-comfort unit, Ma'am.

JAYA   Won't she have to – to –?

AGENT 1   We have a full-recycling and bio-feed-in processor! Your relative will have no further need of the outside world from now 'till... *(He coughs)* ...'till she chooses to de-link.

JAYA   Does she? How will she? –

AGENT 1   Everything is now in the customer's operation, Ma'am. The unit is fully self-sufficient.

JAYA   Won't I have to switch it on or off? No food? No water?

AGENT 1   Total self-sufficiency, Ma'am! There is nothing to be done! *(The other two Agents are ready to leave)* Ma'am, installation is complete.

JAYA   No, wait... who's paying for this thing?

AGENT 1   Debited from the customer's InterPlanta account Ma'am. *(He brings out his card)* ...but in case you have any queries Ma'am, please get in touch with our local representative. *(He hands her the card, turns and leaves)*

JAYA   No, you've not explained anything...What happens if there's a malfunction? *(But there is no one to answer her. She looks around for Om. She sees that he is just about finished tying a bundle together. She goes to him)* Om?

OM   I'm going. Back to InterPlanta. Don't try and stop me.

JAYA   Ohh, let it be now. They've taken Jeetu and there's nothing we could do about it.

OM   No! They'll see their mistake if I go there myself. It's my only chance. What's left for me here? *(He picks up the bundle)* I'll go to them. They took me once, they'll take me again. *(dusts off his clothes, smartens up)* I'm sure they will.

JAYA   You're... you're leaving me?

OM   Not alone. Ma's still there. *(He gestures in the direction of the couch)* And you've got the house to look after.

JAYA   But what'll I do? What'll I tell the guards?

OM   Lock the door from the inside and don't open it till I get back.

JAYA   Om... *(She reaches towards him)*

OM   Please! Just let me go.

He exits. Jaya doesn't try to stop him.
Lights fade as she slowly does up all the bolts, then comes back to the centre of the room, finally folding herself down beside the couch, looking dazed and lost.

SCENE 2

Five days later. The room is unchanged. It is night. Jaya has fallen asleep at the table-cum-sarcophagus. She is looking worn out. There are occasional hums of sound from the Video-Couch. With jarring suddenness the warning tone sounds. Jaya startles awake. The Contact Module is ablaze. It no longer displays any images. It hovers over Jaya.

VOICE *(a rich, gravelly male voice)* Zhaya ...

JAYA   Ahhh!

VOICE   Don't be frightened, Zhaya –

JAYA   Who are you? What d'you want?

VOICE   Calm down honey, be easy – shh, shhh –

JAYA   Go away! Leave me alone!

VOICE *(abruptly the Contact Module moves up and away from her)* Okay, Zhaya. If that's what you really want.

The Contact Module moves a comfortable distance away from her. It dims down till it looks like a Japanese paper lantern. The rest of the stage is in darkness. Jaya raises her head. She looks around warily. There is a pregnant silence.

JAYA Have you gone?

VOICE No.

JAYA *(waits to hear more before speaking again)* Hello?

VOICE I'm here, Zhaya. If you're ready to speak to me.

JAYA Who are you?

VOICE Let's just say, I'm a friend.

JAYA But I don't know you!

VOICE Still – I'm a friend.

JAYA How can you be, if we've never met!

VOICE I've seen you. Heard your voice.

JAYA You mean, you're a friend of Ginni's?

VOICE Sort of, yeah.

JAYA Huh! This is madness! Talking to a lighted ball!

VOICE Why don't I tell you my name?

JAYA It's not natural, any of it!

VOICE Virgil. That's my name, Zhaya and I can show you myself too, if you want –

JAYA I don't want to see you! I don't want to start thinking of you as a real person, when all the time you're just a voice in the air!

VIRGIL Not just my face. All of me.

JAYA You'll come *here*? In *person*?

VIRGIL Sort of. A version of me.

JAYA No! I'm not interested in *versions*. I'm not like Jeetu.

(handwritten annotation) only one that's still in control) tragedy (not really) bc she survives bt it's ambivalent

VIRGIL   Tell you what. I'll show you what I look like.
Then you decide.

JAYA   No! I'll never pluck my eyes out or get into a
box–

VIRGIL   Nothing like that. You'll see me here, with your
own eyes.

JAYA   How? You'll send a statue with the guards?

VIRGIL   Just come to the Module –

*The Contact Module moves till it's within her reach. She
flinches.*

JAYA   This? You'll come from this?

VIRGIL   Don't worry! It can't harm you.

JAYA   No, but –

VIRGIL   It's very simple. Just do as I say. Reach under the
Module –

JAYA   I'm not touching that thing!

VIRGIL   Zhaya, honey, when you see what I look like, I
guarantee, you're gonna be very happy!

JAYA *(turns away from the Module)* No!

VIRGIL   Come on, Zhaya, be a good girl now. I promise
you'll feel better once you see what I look like ... *(when she
refuses to turn)* Aaahhh, all right, then! I guess I'll just
have to do it myself.

*Behind Jaya's back, the Contact Module grows bright, sinks to
floor level, making clicking, whirring sounds. When it rises
again, a projection appears beneath it. A figure is revealed,
first its feet, then its bare legs... it is Jeetu. There is no visor
across his eyes, he looks completely healed. But his expression
is unfamiliar and his haircut, the skimpy clothes he wears, the
way he holds himself – all of these suggest a transformation
that goes beyond mere well-being. He stands still, saying*

nothing, waiting for Jaya to turn. His skin glows slightly. Jaya is bathed in the unearthly radiance emanating from him. She fidgets, knowing that she must avoid turning around. Behind her, the figure crouches down, so that his head is level with hers. She can no longer bear the suspense. She turns.

JAYA   Hhhhhh! Jeetu?

VIRGIL *(the voice comes from the Module though Jeetu's mouth moves)* Well? What d'ya say now!

JAYA   But... you're not – where's that thing across his eyes – he can't be – No! It can't be – it *can't* be him! *(To the Module)* What have you done! It can't be him!

VIRGIL   Oh! You're not happy? Don't you like the way I look?

JAYA   What is this *thing* in front of me! What have you done with – *Jeetu! Jeetu!* What have they done to you! Where have you gone!!

VIRGIL   This *is* me, Zhaya – don't you recognize me? I'm your Jittoo now –

JAYA   Ohhh! *(sobs)*

VIRGIL   I thought you'd be happy to see me!

JAYA   How can I be happy with a ghost?

VIRGIL   I'm not a ghost –

JAYA   You *can't* be who you look like –

VIRGIL   But I am, in one sense.

JAYA   You can't be. It's all just another madness.

VIRGIL   Why, Zhaya? Trust your eyes –

JAYA   But *you're* not here! And *he's* dead... isn't he? The one who owned this... body?

VIRGIL   Depends. On how you define death.

JAYA   There's only one way to define death!

VIRGIL   Not where I live. The body you knew is still alive. He was willing to sell and I was willing to buy –

JAYA   And you paid him in – in – *(She stops, realizing her mistake)* But... it wasn't you! It was... *Ginni?*

VIRGIL   What do you think, Zhaya?

JAYA   Ginni was...

VIRGIL   Nothing. Nobody. A computer-animated wet-dream. I'll show you, just a minute – *(a faint buzz, then the voice that issues from the Module is in Ginni's cloying tones)* Hello Zhaya! Recognize me now? This is what I sound like when my voice is a few decibels higher –

JAYA *(leaps to her feet)* But then Jeetu was paid in phantoms!

VIRGIL *(standing as well)* He sees what he wants to see. He lives what he wants to live.

JAYA   But he has no body!

VIRGIL   He has a casing.

JAYA   – but no body!

VIRGIL   He's happy, Zhaya. He made his choice –

JAYA   I saw his choosing! With his mind bandaged in dreams!

VIRGIL   Was it any worse than his life? When he was lying on the streets... was that better?

JAYA   When he was lying on the streets at least he knew what he was! He was... *(She stops)* But we never told Ginni any of this –

VIRGIL   You did. I listened in to you, Zhaya. I heard every word said in the room. Even when the Module was off, it recorded –

JAYA   Hhhhh!

VIRGIL   I know that Jittoo's not Auwm and that Auwm's your husband.

JAYA   And about Jeetu being...

VIRGIL   ... diseased. Yes, but he was more available than his brother. So we took him.

JAYA   And it doesn't matter! It makes no difference!

VIRGIL   Do I look unwell?

(handwritten margin note: unfair to trade / give up vitality)

JAYA   And you heard every… everything?

VIRGIL   Saw too.

JAYA   Why should I believe you!

VIRGIL   Zhaya, *you've* lied to me – but *I've* told you only the truth.

JAYA   They said you'd be old! And sick!

VIRGIL   I am old and I was sick, until I got into this young body –

JAYA   They said you were a man –

VIRGIL   And I am! Always have been –

JAYA   But then you *looked* like a woman! You *spoke* like a woman –

VIRGIL   Without being one. Without ever saying I was one.

JAYA   You said you wanted Om!

VIRGIL   I didn't ask for Auwm. He came to us.

JAYA   You said you wanted a healthy body –

VIRGIL   Yes, Zhaya – yours!

JAYA   *Mine?* But it was Om who got the job!

VIRGIL   We're interested in women, where I live, Zhaya. Child-bearing women.

JAYA   But...

VIRGIL   Om was part of the job, but not all of it. We look for young couples, without children –

JAYA   ... Om said he wasn't married!

VIRGIL   His polygraph showed he lied. All donors lie. They think we need singles, they think we need men and only the very desperate apply. That suits us just fine, cos' unless they're desperate, they won't do as we say. We search for skin and blood matches. Auwm matched mine.

JAYA   Yet you've taken *Jeetu's* body!

VIRGIL   Jittoo is Auwm's brother. He was an even better match.

Succumb to women's right being taken away) (handwritten margin note)

JAYA   I don't know what to believe!

VIRGIL   We look for young men's bodies to live in and
young women's bodies in which to sow their children –

JAYA   What about your own!

VIRGIL   We lost the art of having children.

JAYA   How can it be?

VIRGIL   We began to live longer and longer. And healthier
each generation. And more demanding... soon there was
competition between one generation and the next – old
against young, parent against child. We older ones had the
advantage of experience. We prevailed. But our victory
was bitter. We secured Paradise at the cost of birds and
flowers, bees and snakes! So we designed this programme.
We support poorer sections of the world, while gaining
fresh bodies for ourselves.

JAYA   And it works? You live forever?

VIRGIL   Not everyone can take it. We fixed the car, but
not the driver! I'm one of the stubborn ones. This is my
fourth body in fifty years.

JAYA   Fourth!

VIRGIL   Two were not successful. It hasn't been easy,
Zhaya. I won't hide that from you. But so long as I can
afford to keep trying – I will!

JAYA *(trying to find arguments for resisting)* But I've never
been with child.

VIRGIL   I know I can fill your belly.

JAYA *(drops her gaze)* No ...

VIRGIL   You've longed for a child. Your arms cry out for
that sweet burden. To hold it in your arms, to cuddle and
crush it with kisses –

JAYA   No... it was never meant to be. Years ago, a seer
told me, my stars denied it –

VIRGIL   Yet I sanction it now, I do! With Jittoo's body –

JAYA   Jeetu's dead and you're a... a phantom!

VIRGIL   Honey, I'm real and warm and willing – this body which once belonged to Jittoo now contains a red-blooded all-American man! This body is hot with life and heavy with desire! This body aches for you and to give you what you yearn for –

JAYA   A married woman must not hear such words from a stranger's mouth –

VIRGIL   This mouth is no stranger to you, Zhaya – my voice is but the latest tenant in a house that you have known.

JAYA   No!

VIRGIL   Can you deny the truth that is throbbing in my newly commissioned veins?

JAYA   Please – ohh, it's madness you're offering me –

VIRGIL   Is it madness to offer you your heart's desire?

JAYA   I'd stopped hoping –

VIRGIL   You can start again. I'm here to make it possible.

JAYA   But whose child would it be? Jeetu's? Or... yours?

VIRGIL   This is Jittoo's body!

JAYA   Yes, but –

VIRGIL   It would belong to this body – Jittoo's body –

JAYA   But would it be Jeetu's *child*? Would it look like him? Have his voice?

VIRGIL   No one can say for certain which parent a child will take after. It could look like you, after all, have your voice.

JAYA   Yes – but –
(She extends a hand towards the apparition – there is a crackle as her hand passes through it. She recoils) Ohhh!

VIRGIL   Ah-ah! Can't touch!

JAYA   Then – how?

There is a knocking at the door.

GUARD 1   InterPlanta Services! Request permission to make contact!

VIRGIL   Don't be frightened! It's just the agency. I can tell them to wait, if you want –

JAYA   Wait for what!

VIRGIL   The guards will make the child possible, Zhaya. It's just a formality, a device –

JAYA   Device?

VIRGIL   You know, an implant. Something I sent, which they're ready to deliver. And you can take your time. About three days are still within your fertile cycle –

JAYA   What are you talking about?

VIRGIL   Zhaya, I'd love to travel to be with you, but I can't.

JAYA   You who are so powerful, you who can travel from body to body –

VIRGIL   The environment you live in is too polluted for me, Zhaya –

JAYA   Then you are a phantom, after all. An illusion come to mock me – again! *(She tries to strike the Module, but it flicks out of her reach)*

VIRGIL   I'll take you through the procedure, step by step. It's simple and it's painless.

JAYA *(still trying to hit the globe)* No! The pain tells me that I'm alive. I want the pain!

VIRGIL   Then you can have all the pain you want, Zhaya – just as you want. It can take the usual nine months if you want, with diet and exercise and medical personnel to monitor you –

JAYA *(starts throwing things at the Module, roaring in frustration)* Aarrrrhhhhhhhh!

VIRGIL   I'll be with you, all the way.

JAYA   You're *not* here! Jeetu's dead and I'm alone –

VIRGIL　　I can set it up so that we can be together, go places, anywhere you want – right inside your room.

JAYA　　I don't want your make-believe travels!

VIRGIL　　Zhaya we can even be... intimate! Really. But I thought you'd like to get to know me first –

JAYA　　I want real hands touching me. I want to feel a real weight upon me – *(looking around for things to throw)*

VIRGIL　　And it's all possible –

JAYA　　No! Not without risking your skin! Never! Do you hear me, whoever you are, whatever you are? Never! Never! *Never!* There is no closeness without risk! *(With this, she manages to get a direct hit. There is a shower of sparks and a crack of electric light. The Contact Module abruptly switches off, the whole room flickers in purple and blue light. When the light stabilizes again, the figure of Jeetu is gone. Looking up, towards the darkened globe)* You! Can you hear me?

From the door, a knocking.

GUARD 1 *(through the door)* InterPlanta Services! Request permission to enter!

JAYA *(To the Module)* Look, I've understood you now. I know you're stronger than me, you're richer than me. But if you want me, you must risk your skin to get me. Even though it's really Jeetu's skin – I want you to risk it!

GUARD 1 *(hammering at the door)* Madam! Madam! We have an urgent message for you from your Receiver!

JAYA　　Either that or–

GUARD 1 *(sounds of mechanical activity at the door)* ...attaching external speaker ...

There is a scraping sound, a crackle.

virgil loses
the child /time (handwritten in left margin)

JAYA *(grabs up a piece of broken glass)* … you won't have me at all!

GUARD 1   Speaker installed. Begin transmission...

VIRGIL *(his voice crackles through the door)* Zhaya, listen to me – you can't hope to win against me!

JAYA   I've discovered a new definition for winning. Winning by losing. I win if you lose.

VIRGIL   Zhaya, this is childish!

JAYA   It's your fault. You took everything I care about away from me. So I *can't* lose any more! I've got nothing left to lose.

VIRGIL   But your life, Zhaya! That's still ahead of you!

JAYA   Huh, my life! It's not really mine any more. You've shown me that. The only thing I have which is really mine now is my death. My death and my pride.

VIRGIL   Pride! Pride is nothing! A poor man's fancy dress.

JAYA   And if I let you take it from me, I will be naked as well as poor! You'll never let me have what you have! You'll only share your electronic dreams with me, your *'virtual'* touch, your plastic shadows – no! If the only clothes I can afford are these rags of pride then I'll wear them with my head held high!

VIRGIL   Zhaya, don't make me tell the guards to force the door… if you want respect, then open the door yourself.

JAYA   You can't see me, can you? I'm holding a piece of glass against my throat. If you force the door, you'll push this glass into my throat.

VIRGIL   Zhaya, please! We've got this far…I love your spirit, I really do. In these months and weeks, I've come to admire you and care for you. Don't let me down now!

JAYA   Then risk your skin.

VIRGIL   You're being unreasonable!

JAYA   Is it unreasonable to ask one who has cheated death, to cross the oceans?

VIRGIL   Zhaya…

JAYA   I'm bored of this argument! Don't you understand? This game is over! Either you have to erase me and start again or... accept a different set of rules.

VIRGIL   You're not stupid, Zhaya – you know it's impossible to win against me.

JAYA   Stupid or not, if I lose my life, I win this game.

VIRGIL   You won't be alive to savour that victory.

JAYA   But I'll die knowing that you, who live only to win, will have lost to a poor, weak and helpless woman. And I'll get more pleasure out of that first moment of death than I've had in my entire life so far!

VIRGIL   Zhaya …

JAYA   You still can't see me, can you?

VIRGIL   No, but–

JAYA   That's all right, I'll tell you what I'm doing. *(matches her actions to her words)* I'm collecting all the pills and medicines I can find. I'm going to take the ones for staying awake, until I run out of them. And if I don't hear the sound of your own hand on my door before that time, I'll take my life. If the guards cause me any discomfort whatsoever – I'll take my life. If you do anything other than come here in person – I'll take my life!

VIRGIL   Zhaya – this is wrong, this is ridiculous.

JAYA *(unperturbed)* And in the meantime, I want you to practice saying my name correctly. It's Jaya – *'J'* as in justice, *'J'* as in jam.

VIRGIL   Zhaya…

JAYA   I won't talk to you unless you say it right!

VIRGIL *(pause)* Zha... Zh... Jaya… Jaya… Jaya, listen to me.

JAYA   No! You listen to me! I want to be left alone, truly alone. I don't want to hear any sounds, I don't want any disturbances. I'm going to take my pills, watch TV, have a dozen baths a day, eat for three instead of one. For

the first time in my life and maybe the last time of my life –
I'm going to enjoy myself, all by myself. *(A beat)* I suggest
you take some rest. You have a long journey ahead of you
and it's sure to be a hard one.

*Lights fade out as Jaya settles down comfortably in front of the
television, bolstered by cushions. She looks happy and relaxed.
She points the remote and turns the sound up loud. Rich,
joyous music fills the room.*

The end.

> Satisfied / happy bc she's in control
> → watching TV dangerous b/
> she knows it's all fake
> → information literate

Manjula Padmanabhan

A writer and artist living in New Delhi, she has
illustrated twenty-one books for children and drew a
daily comic strip called *SUKI* for six years. She has also
published a collection of short stories entitled *Hot Death,
Cold Soup* (Kali for Women). Her two most recent books
are *Getting There* (Picador) a fictionalised memoir and
This is SUKI! (Duckfoot Press) an album of her comic
strip.

Harvest is her fifth play.

> key themes
> - capitalism dehumanizes (human capital stock)
>   → uses media to lie(brainwash us
> - neo-colonialism is new imperalism
> - exploitation
> - cultural hegemony